The flawed and the flawless

JUDGES

by Timothy Keller

Editor: Carl Laferton

Judges For You

If you are reading *Judges For You* (see page 77) alongside this Good Book Guide, here is how the studies in this booklet link to the chapters of Judges For You:

Study One > Ch 1–2
Study Two > Ch 3–4
Study Three > Ch 5–7

Study Four > Ch 7–8
Study Five > Ch 9–11
Study Six > Ch 12–13

The flawed and the flawless
The Good Book Guide to Judges
© Timothy Keller, 2013. Reprinted 2014, 2015, 2016
Series Consultants: Tim Chester, Tim Thornborough,
    Anne Woodcock, Carl Laferton

The Good Book Company
Tel (UK): 0333 123 0880
Tel (US): 866 244 2165
Tel (int): + (44) 208 942 0880
Email: admin@thegoodbook.co.uk

Websites
North America: www.thegoodbook.com
UK: www.thegoodbook.co.uk
Australia: www.thegoodbook.com.au
New Zealand: www.thegoodbook.co.nz

ISBN: 9781908762887

Printed in the Czech Republic

CONTENTS

Introduction: Good Book Guides

Every Bible-study group is different—yours may take place in a church building, in a home or in a cafe, on a train, over a leisurely mid-morning coffee or squashed into a 30-minute lunch break. Your group may include new Christians, mature Christians, non-Christians, moms and tots, students, businessmen or teens. That's why we've designed these *Good Book Guides* to be flexible for use in many different situations.

Our aim in each session is to uncover the meaning of a passage, and see how it fits into the "big picture" of the Bible. But that can never be the end. We also need to appropriately apply what we have discovered to our lives. Let's take a look at what is included:

⊕ **Talkabout:** Most groups need to "break the ice" at the beginning of a session, and here's the question that will do that. It's designed to get people talking around a subject that will be covered in the course of the Bible study.

⊕ **Investigate:** The Bible text for each session is broken up into manageable chunks, with questions that aim to help you understand what the passage is about. **The Leader's Guide** contains **guidance on questions**, and sometimes ⊗ additional "follow-up" questions.

⊕ **Explore more (optional):** These questions will help you connect what you have learned to other parts of the Bible, so you can begin to fit it all together like a jig-saw; or occasionally look at a part of the passage that's not dealt with in detail in the main study.

⊕ **Apply:** As you go through a Bible study, you'll keep coming across **apply** sections. These are questions to get the group discussing what the Bible teaching means in practice for you and your church. ⊙ **Getting personal** is an opportunity for you to think, plan and pray about the changes that you personally may need to make as a result of what you have learned.

⊕ **Pray:** We want to encourage prayer that is rooted in God's word—in line with his concerns, purposes and promises. So each session ends with an opportunity to review the truths and challenges highlighted by the Bible study, and turn them into prayers of request and thanksgiving.

The **Leader's Guide** and introduction provide historical background information, explanations of the Bible texts for each session, ideas for **optional extra** activities, and guidance on how best to help people uncover the truths of God's word.

Why study Judges?

Judges can be described as "despicable people doing deplorable things." It is a history of (few) highs and (more) lows; of murder, assassination and massacres; of immorality, lawlessness and unfaithfulness.

It is the story of some of the Bible's most familiar "heroes": Samson, Gideon, Deborah; as well as some of its more unsung ones: Othniel, Barak, Jael. It tells of how Israel's "judges" saved the people over and over again from the cruel oppression of the nations around them.

Yet as the history unfolds, the "heroes" become increasingly flawed and failing. They do many appalling things, and the efforts bring about less and less good. Really, they are hardly heroes at all. Judges is a dismal story—and it is all true.

So as we read it, we will be led to ask, repeatedly: *What in the world is this doing in the Bible?*

And the answer is crucial. It is the gospel! Judges (like the rest of the Bible) is not a book of virtues; it is not a series of inspirational stories to imitate; it will not present us with a moral code. It *is* about the God of mercy and long-suffering, who continually works in and through and for his people; and who does so despite his people's constant resistance to his purposes, both then and now.

Ultimately, we will only find one hero in this book—and he's God.

We'll read of how he rescued Israel from the mess that they made by worshiping the gods of the people who lived around and among them. We'll learn from the mistakes of God's people as they lived in a time which offered them a great variety of alternative "gods" to love and serve and trust—a time not so different from our own. And we'll be thrilled as we see, in the men and women God used to rescue and rule his people, dim shadows of the One who God would send finally to lead us.

Judges is not an easy read. But as God's people, living in the era we do, it is an essential one.

One last word. There are six studies, covering all 21 chapters of Judges. That is a lot to cover! You will get much more out of your times together if you each read through the section individually before you meet.

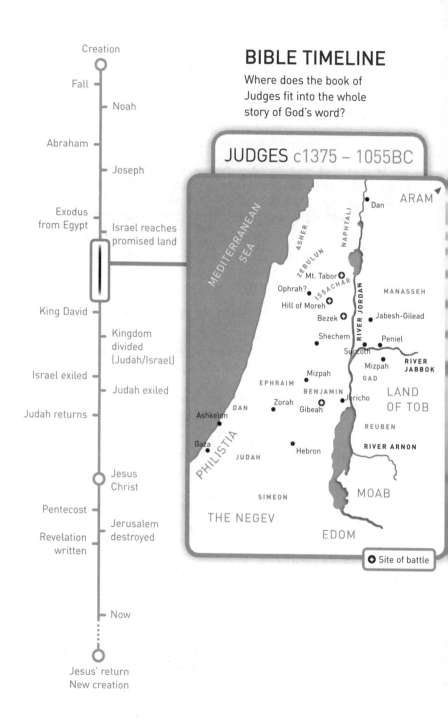

BIBLE TIMELINE

Where does the book of Judges fit into the whole story of God's word?

Creation
Fall
Noah
Abraham
Joseph
Exodus from Egypt
Israel reaches promised land
King David
Kingdom divided (Judah/Israel)
Israel exiled
Judah exiled
Judah returns
Jesus Christ
Pentecost
Jerusalem destroyed
Revelation written
Now
Jesus' return
New creation

JUDGES c1375 – 1055BC

MEDITERRANEAN SEA

ARAM

Dan

ASHER
ZEBULUN
NAPHTALI
ISSACHAR
Mt. Tabor
Ophrah?
Hill of Moreh
Bezek
Shechem
Succoth
MANASSEH
Jabesh-Gilead
Peniel
RIVER JORDAN

Mizpah
EPHRAIM
BENJAMIN
Zorah
Gibeah
Jericho
Mizpah
GAD
RIVER JABBOK
LAND OF TOB

Ashkelon
DAN
REUBEN

Gaza
JUDAH
Hebron
RIVER ARNON

PHILISTIA

SIMEON
THE NEGEV
MOAB

EDOM

⊕ Site of battle

1

Judges 1 v 1 – 3 v 6

A SHAKY START

⊕ talkabout

1. Why do things go wrong in churches?

⬇ investigate

As we'll see, the book of Judges begins by pointing us back to Joshua…

❯ Read Joshua 1 v 1-9; 23 v 3-13

2. What does God command Israel to do, both in Joshua's time and after he has died?

   • What must not they *not* do?

❯ Read Judges 1 v 1-36

3. How well does Israel obey God's commands in:

   • v 1-2?

   • v 3 (note what God had said in verse 2)?

- v 4-11?

- v 19-21?

- v 22-26?

- v 27-33?

- v 34-36?

4. Make a list of the reasons given (or hinted at) why the tribes of Israel failed to settle in all the land God had promised them, pushing the Canaanites out.

5. What examples of whole-hearted obedience do verses 12-16 show us?

⤳ apply

6. How does this episode show us the difference between common sense and faithful obedience?

🔅 getting personal

It is not our lack of strength that prevents us from enjoying God's blessings, and which means we do not worship God wholeheartedly; it is our lack of faith in *his* strength. Othniel attacked a city in God's strength; the tribe of Judah concluded they couldn't manage it.

Can you think of times in your life you have been brave because of your faith?

When do you find it hardest to follow God's commands instead of your own "common sense." Why?

⬇ investigate

Chapter 1 represents Israel's perspective on the campaign, their "press releases" on what happened. In summary, the Israelites said: "We could not drive them out."

> ❱ **Read Judges 2 v 1-5**

7. What is God's verdict on the same episode (v 1-3)?

> **DICTIONARY**
>
> **Covenant (v 1-2):** binding agreement, or set of promises.
> **Altars (v 2):** places for making sacrifices to a god.

8. What is the tension between what God had said before (v 1), and what he says now (v 3)?

God is saying: *You have put me in an impossible situation. I have sworn to bless you as my beloved people, and sworn not to bless you as disobedient people. I have promised to love you as my people; but I have also promised that I will judge sin. How am I to solve this dilemma?*

9. **Read Romans 3 v 23-26 and 2 Corinthians 5 v 21.** How did God solve the dilemma, so that he could be both just *and* forgiving to his people?

❯ Read Judges 2 v 6 – 3 v 6

This section should be seen as a "second introduction" to the book of Judges. We need to have both 1 v 1 – 2 v 5 *and* 2 v 6 – 3 v 6 in mind as we read through the rest of the book.

10. What cycle in Israelite history do verses 10-21 summarize?

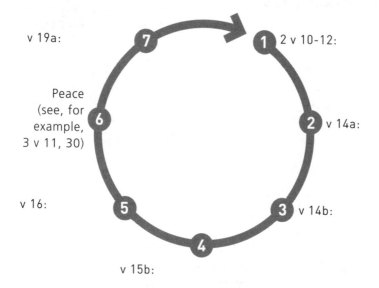

v 19a:

Peace (see, for example, 3 v 11, 30)

v 16:

v 15b:

7

6

5

4

1 2 v 10-12:

2 v 14a:

3 v 14b:

⊡ explore more

Compare 2 v 7 and v 10-11. Within a generation, Israel had gone from being people who "served the LORD" to people who "served the Baals." There is no automatic passing of faith from one generation to the next, from parents to children.

> **Read Deuteronomy 6 v 4-9, 20-25**

What do we need to do to pass our faith on to the next generation?

⊖ apply

11. How might we say: "I could not" but God says: "You would not," when it comes to:

• forgiveness?

• telling the truth / sharing the gospel?

• being tempted?

⊡ getting personal

How does the reality of your sin and of God's grace prompt you to praise and thank him today?

Are there areas where you say to God: "I cannot" but the truth is you will not? What would change if you had whole-hearted faith in him?

↑ pray

Thank God for his promises to his people, then and now. Thank God that, through the cross, he keeps his promises to bless us, despite our sinfulness. Thank God that he challenges us to see where our "can'ts" are in fact "won'ts."

Ask God to show you where you need to obey him wholeheartedly. Ask him to give you the trust in him which will enable you to do so. Speak to him about any other ways this study has excited or challenged you.

2 Judges 3 v 7 – 5 v 31
OTHNIEL, EHUD, DEBORAH: EXPECT THE UNEXPECTED

The story so far

Israel is living in the land God promised, but alongside people who worship false gods, because they didn't fully trust God and so didn't fully obey him.

⊕ talkabout

1. What stops people taking risks?

⊕ investigate

> Read Judges 3 v 7-11

2. How do we see each stage of the "Judges cycle" in Othniel's story?

DICTIONARY

Asherahs (v 7): false goddesses worshiped by the Canaanites.

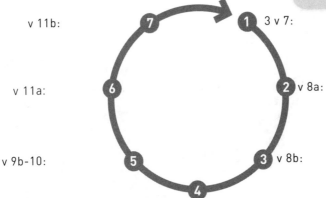

v 11b:

v 11a:

v 9b-10:

7

6

5

1 3 v 7:

2 v 8a:

3 v 8b:

4

v 9a:

❯ Read Judges 3 v 12-31

3. What are the similarities between the Ehud episode, and the one featuring Othniel?

This time, the man God uses to save his people from oppression is "left-handed" (v 15). Since most people were right-handed, and it was the hand you held your sword in, the right hand was a symbol of power and ability. Verse 15 says, literally, that Ehud was "unable to use his right hand"—it is probable that it was paralyzed in some way. God's choice of a left-hander—a handicapped man—would have been greatly surprising to the first readers of Judges.

4. But how does Ehud's weakness enable him to defeat Israel's enemy?

5. **Read Isaiah 53 v 2-6** (a prophecy looking forward to Jesus) and **Luke 23 v 33-39.** How is Ehud a preview of the Lord Jesus?

• **Read 1 Corinthians 1 v 26-29.** How is Ehud a preview of every follower of the Lord Jesus?

⊙ apply

6. How is knowing that we are "left-handed":

• humbling?

• freeing?

• How will remembering and rejoicing that we are "left-handed" change our Christian lives?

⊡ getting personal

If we try to ignore our spiritual weakness, we'll never appreciate our salvation, or enjoy relying on God's power in, and plan for, our lives.

How regularly do you consider the ways in which you were, and are, spiritually weak?

Are there ways in which you could enjoy living for God, but you're holding back because you're "not good enough"?

⊡ investigate

▶ Read Judges 4 v 1-24

7. How is Deborah like Othniel and Ehud?

DICTIONARY

Prophetess (v 4): God's messenger, through whom he spoke to His people..
Kenite (v 11): a descendant of Moses' in-laws (see 1 v 16).

• How is she different?

There are two ways of understanding Deborah and Barak's conversation in verses 6-9. One is that in verse 8, Barak is *lacking faith*—and so although Deborah agrees to go with him (v 9), he won't get the honor for the victory because of his timid lack of faith in God's promise and command.

The other option is that Barak is actually *showing faith* by asking Deborah, God's spokesperson, to go with him; and that in verse 9, Deborah is saying: "On the expedition you are taking, the honor will not be yours" (see NIV footnote). She is making a statement about his future, not giving a verdict on his faith. I favor the latter reading—it fits better with Hebrews 11 v 32-34, where Barak is called a hero of the faith.

8. On this second reading, how does Barak show us what real faith is?

9. How does Deborah's prophecy in verse 9 come true?

> **Read Judges 5 v 1-31**

These are the same events, from a different angle. This is a song, and is more theological, looking under the surface.

10. How does this chapter picture the battle between Barak's men and Sisera's forces (v 4-5, 19-22)?

DICTIONARY

Blessed (v 24): here, meaning "praised for being part of God's purposes."
Girl (v 30): literally, a female sex-slave.

• What does it tell us about why Israel won the battle?

⊡ explore more

optional

How do you feel about what Jael did (4 v 18-22)? What was good? What was not good?
How does 5 v 24 describe her?
How would you square this with Jesus' command to love, pray for and bless our enemies in our personal relationships (Luke 6 v 27-28)? How do the following passages help us in thinking through how we should view our enemies?
• *Revelation 11 v 15-18*
• *Romans 12 v 14, 19-20*
• *Acts 17 v 31*
• *Luke 23 v 34*

⊟ apply

11. It's Thursday morning, and David is at his office with five other guys, none of them Christians. His wife, Maria, is meeting some friends, none of whom are Christians. The sermon at their church on Sunday is: "Why bother with Jesus?" They have invitations in their pockets.

In what ways do they need to have each of the three aspects of faith that Barak did (see Question Eight)?

• Think about what will happen if they forget one of them.

12. What happens when we have only a Judges-4 "surface-level" perspective on our lives, and forget to combine it with a Judges-5 "theological" perspective? Why is it easy to do this?

⊡ getting personal

In which aspect of faith do you find you are weakest? Will you pray for God to grow your faith, and ask for opportunities to live by it?

Are there ways in which God is calling you to take risks for him as he wins his victories?

⊡ pray

Thank God for:

• saving you through his "left-handed" rescuer, Jesus.

• saving you despite your "left-handedness."

• being willing to use you to achieve his purposes. (Perhaps thank him for specific ways he has done, and is doing, this in your lives.)

Ask God:

• to help you to have Barak-like faith.

• to enable you to live with a Judges-5 perspective; and to encourage one another to do so.

• to inspire you to take risks as you obey God, trusting his promises; and to encourage one another to do so.

3 GIDEON: THE DANGERS OF SUCCESS

Judges 6 v 1 – 8 v 31

The story so far

Israel is living in the land God promised, but alongside people who worship false gods, because they didn't fully trust God and so didn't fully obey him.

God's people rejected him and served other gods; he allowed their enemies to oppress them; he rescued them through his judges—Othniel, Ehud, Deborah.

⊕ talkabout

1. What are the dangers of success?

⬇ investigate

▶ Read Judges 6 v 1-24

2. What is different in this cycle:
   • with the oppression (v 1-6)?

   • with how God responds to the Israelites crying out to him (v 7-10)?

DICTIONARY

Locusts (v 5): large grasshoppers, that sometimes gather in huge swarms eating all the crops in their flight-path.
Impoverished (v 6): brought about a state of total poverty.
Threshing (v 11): separating grain from wheat.

3. What does this suggest about the type of "crying" Israel is doing? Why do the people need a prophet before they have a rescuer?

4. When the angel of the LORD visits Gideon, how do their opinions differ on whether God has forgotten his people (v 13-14)?

• How are both God and Gideon correct about Gideon's ability (v 12, 15)?

📖 **explore more**

optional

Who speaks in v 12 and v 20? Who speaks in v 14, 16, 18? What is strange about this?

How does Gideon react when he realizes who he has been speaking to (v 22)? What does this tell us about who he has seen (see Exodus 33 v 20)?

This angel (literally "messenger") is both the LORD and not the LORD! Who do you think this "angel" is?

❯ **Read Judges 6 v 25-40**

5. How does God enable Gideon to begin to deal with:

• the enemy among God's people (v 25-32)?

• the enemy around God's people (v 33-35)?

• the enemy within Gideon (v 36-40)?

➔ **apply**

6. How is the answer to the second part of Question Four a picture of what it means to be a Christian?

- How are the answers to Question Five a picture of what it means to live as a Christian?

⊕ investigate

❯ **Read Judges 7 v 1-8a**

7. What does God do to Gideon's army?

- What lesson does God want to teach him, and Israel (v 2)?

❯ **Read Judges 7 v 8b-23**

8. How does God reassure Gideon (v 8b-15)?

- How does Gideon's response show that he has received reassurance?

9. How should the manner of the victory (v 16-23) help Gideon and Israel to trust in God, and not boast in themselves?

> **Read Judges 7 v 24 – 8 v 31**

10. Neither Gideon nor Israel has learned "the lesson of the triumph of the 300." How do we see that here in:

• Ephraim?

• the residents of Succoth and Peniel?

• Gideon?

The Israelites have totally failed to remember the lesson of the battle—they think Gideon saved them from their enemies (v 22)! But Gideon knows that the only king Israel should have is the LORD, not him or his son (v 23). The LORD is Israel's true Ruler as well as their true Rescuer.

11. But how do Gideon's actions then not match up with his words?

→ apply

12. What do we learn from Gideon about the dangers of God-given success?

* How is it possible to make the same mistakes today?

13. How does the "Gideon episode" show us that God is great?

⊡ getting personal

Have there been times in the past when God has weakened you so that you can see more clearly that he is the one who saves? How does this move you to praise him?

Are there areas today where your success is tempting you to think you can rely on yourself; or deserve honor from others? What resentful attitudes and/or arrogant behavior is this causing?

When do you most need to remember the "lesson of the 300"?

↑ pray

Thank God for what you have seen of his character and goodness in these chapters.

Speak to God about ways you have been challenged by what you've seen of your own heart and life.

4 Judges 8 v 32 – 12 v 15

ABIMELECH & JEPHTHAH: DARK TIMES

The story so far

Israel is living in the land God promised, but alongside people who worship false gods, because they didn't fully trust God and so didn't fully obey him.

God's people rejected him and served other gods; he allowed their enemies to oppress them; he rescued them through his judges—Othniel, Ehud, Deborah.

God strengthened Gideon as judge, then weakened the army to teach that victory was his. Gideon didn't learn this, and acted as king in God's place.

⊕ talkabout

1. What makes for bad leadership?

⊥ investigate

▶ **Read Judges 8 v 32 – 10 v 5**

2. How is Abimelech different from the judges who have come before his time?

> **DICTIONARY**
>
> **Inclined (9 v 3):** willing, persuaded.
> **Millstone (10 v 53):** a very heavy circular stone used for grinding grain.

In v 7-20, Abimelech's surviving half-brother, Jotham, challenges him. His point is that Abimelech (like the thornbush) is not fit to rule. Thornbushes were only a foot or two tall, and caught fire very easily—so they gave no shade or protection to the other trees, and were a danger to them.

So Jotham curses Abimelech, and the men of Shechem, saying in verses 16-20: *If you've been fair to Gideon's family in making Abimelech your king (and let's face it, you haven't but if you have), then may you find great blessing in the rule of King Abimelech. But if you haven't (and, let's face it, you haven't), then I hope you and he get what you all deserve—you burned by him, and he burned by you.*

But for three years, nothing happens, and Abimelech rules (v 22)...

3. What brings Abimelech down?

• v 23:

• v 26-29:

• v 50-55:

• v 56-57:

• If you had been an Israelite at the time, which of these could you have seen? Which would you not have known about?

During the rule of Abimelech, Israel plumbs new depths. Yet "after the time of Abimelech ... Tola ... rose to save Israel." But no enemy is named—who did Tola rise to save Israel from?

4. How does chapter 9 show us the answer to that question?

• What does it show us is the greatest problem God's people have?

⊡ getting personal

This is the sheer grace of God. In Jesus, God saves us from ourselves—from the failings and ambitions of our hearts, and from the divisions and strife among us.

In what ways has God saved you from yourself?

⊖ apply

5. Paul says in Romans 1 v 18: "The wrath of God is being revealed from heaven against all the godlessness and wickedness of men who suppress the truth by their wickedness." What does the story of Abimelech show us about God's present judgment?

• How is this encouraging for us today?

⊍ investigate

▶ **Read Judges 10 v 6 – 11 v 33**

Again, Israel rejects God and worships idols. Again, God allows enemies to shatter, crush and oppress them. Again, they cry out to God for rescue.

6. How does God respond (10 v 11-14)? What does he want the people to realize in verse 14, do you think?

• How does verse 16 show that Israel have understood?

☺ **getting personal**

Until verse 16, Israel said "sorry" to God while hanging on to their idols. They changed their behavior, but not their hearts.

Are there any idols you are quietly loving and serving alongside God? How are you being challenged to get rid of "foreign gods"?

How does knowing that God has compassion on those who really turn to him motivate you to commit to loving him alone?

7. How does the Gileadites' treatment of Jephthah, God's chosen judge, mirror their treatment of God?

▶ **Read Judges 11 v 34 – 12 v 15**

DICTIONARY

Renegades (12 v 4): deserters, outcasts, rejects.

Notice that Jephthah seeks a peaceful resolution before taking up his sword.

How does he respond to the king of Ammon's claim that part of Israel's land used to belong to the Ammonites:
- *in 11 v 15-22?*
- *in verses 23-24?*
- *in verses 25-27?*
How does the king of Ammon respond (v 28)?

▶ **Read 1 Peter 2 v 21-25**

How are Jephthah and Jesus examples of the way we should respond to unfair accusations?

Until now, once a judge has won victory over Israel's enemies, there has been "peace." But not here.

8. What happens, instead, and why:
- in Jephthah's family (1 v 30-31, 34-39)?

- within the people of Israel (12 v 1-6)?

9. Why do you think Jephthah made the vow in the first place?

• Why do you think he kept the vow in such a horrific way?

→ apply

10. What are the lessons for us from Jephthah's family tragedy?

11. What are the lessons for us from Ephraim's tragedy?

12. How do these two dark episodes in Israel's history show us how wonderful God is?

↑ pray

Use your answers to Question Twelve to prompt your **praise of God**.

Use your answers to Questions Ten and Eleven to shape your **prayers to God**.

5 Judges 13–16
SAMSON: A SHADOW IN THE DARKNESS

The story so far

God's people rejected him and served other gods; he allowed their enemies to oppress them; he rescued them through his judges—Othniel, Ehud, Deborah.

God strengthened Gideon as judge, then weakened the army to teach that victory was his. Gideon didn't learn this, and acted as king in God's place.

God judged Abimelech through the outworking of his sin. God used Jephthah to save Israel, but his pagan beliefs had tragic consequences for his family.

⊕ talkabout

1. Why do people disobey God?

⊔ investigate

> **Read Judges 13 v 1-25**

The cycle begins: Israel does evil, they're handed over...

2. What should happen next, but doesn't?

> **DICTIONARY**
>
> **Fermented (v 4):** alcoholic.
> **Nazirite (v 5):** see next page.

• What does this tell us about Israel's spiritual state by this time?

• In verse 5, God begins to raise up a judge to deliver his people. Why is this remarkable, given what Israel *hasn't* done?

3. How is Samson's birth similar to Jesus' birth?

4. What does the angel tell Samson's mother about how he is to be brought up (v 4-5)?

The angel is referring to a vow, found in Numbers 6 v 1-21. It involved:
• not cutting your hair.
• not eating or drinking any produce of vines.
• not having contact with any dead body.
It was a sign that you were looking to God with great intensity and focus. The vow was made voluntarily, and for a set period of time; but here, Samson is to be born into this "set-apart" state, and to keep it all his life.

▶ Read Judges 14 v 1 – 16 v 3

5. How well does Samson keep his Nazirite vow?

• How well does he keep God's commands to all his people (look back to Joshua 23 v 9-13)?

6. How do we see that Israel have virtually become Philistines:

• in Samson's attitudes and actions?

• in the tribe of Judah's attitudes and actions?

optional

⊙ explore more

Three times, we're told explicitly that Samson enjoyed Spirit-given strength (14 v 6; 14 v 19; 15 v 14-15).

What does he use that strength to do each time?

We keep seeing the Spirit helping Samson. But why don't we see him growing in holiness? How can he be so empowered by the Spirit and yet show no patience, humility, or self-control?

▶ Read 1 Corinthians 12 v 4-7; 13 v 1-3

What does Paul say here that the Spirit gives?
What must these be accompanied by to stop them being useless?

▶ Read Galatians 5 v 19-25

What does Paul say here that the Spirit gives?
Which work of the Spirit does Samson have? Which doesn't he have? Which is the sign of real spiritual growth? What happens if we forget this?

⇥ apply

7. Why is the church adopting the values and beliefs of the world more dangerous than the world oppressing and persecuting the church?

• How is this danger most acute in your church and your culture?

☺ getting personal

How do you feel the pressure to fit in with the surrounding culture in your own life?

What promises of God could you bring to mind to remind you and enable you to live for him, and not like the world?

⊥ investigate

> **Read Judges 16 v 4-21**

8. How do we see both Samson's priorities and his weaknesses in this section?

• What, ultimately, was the key to Samson's strength (v 19-20)?

➔ apply

The Philistines believed Samson's power was magic—that there must be something he did that kept him strong, and something they could do (tie him with fresh thongs; with new ropes; tie his hair to a loom; shave his head) which would weaken him. Samson believed the power came automatically; that the magic worked regardless of what he did or how he treated God.

In fact, his strength relied only, and completely, on God giving it to him. Spiritual power comes from God being with us, as we seek to follow him in our hearts (see Matthew 28 v 18-20).

9. We may think we don't believe in magic. But think about the question: *Why do I think God will bless me?* How can we make the same mistake as the Philistines?

- How can we make the same mistake as Samson?

- What does it look like to live as a Christian who knows God is the God who gives graciously?

☺ getting personal

The more God blessed Samson, the more Samson grew confident, complacent, and ungodly. In grace, God takes our weaknesses and uses them for us; but in sin, we take even his gifts and strengths and use them against him.

How do these truths about God and about humanity ring true in your own experience, past and present?
Do you need to stop using a blessing for your own ends, and start to use it to serve God?

⊕ investigate

❯ **Read Judges 16 v 22-31**

10. How does Samson at last show faithful reliance on God?

• What does it cost him to fulfil his mission?

11. How does Samson's victory point us to the cross of Jesus?

• How is what Jesus did in his death even greater?

➔ apply

12. What does Samson teach us about how not to follow God?!

• What does the Samson episode teach us about how kind God is?

⬆ pray

Praise God for the truths about Jesus that Samson points you to. **Thank God** for the ways Jesus is greater than Samson. **Ask God** to enable you to use each blessing he's given each of you to obey him and serve him.

6

Judges 17 – 21
"ISRAEL HAD NO KING"

The story so far

Israel rejected God, serving other gods; he allowed their enemies to oppress them; he rescued them through his judges—Othniel, Ehud, Deborah, Gideon.

God judged Abimelech through the outworking of his sin. God used Jephthah to save Israel, but his pagan beliefs had tragic consequences for his family.

Samson and Israel were no different from their enemies; but God used Samson, in his death, to begin to rescue his people from ceasing to be his people.

⊕ talkabout

1. If you had to sum up humans in one word, what would it be?

⊕ investigate

In some ways, the end of Samson is the end of the Judges story. He is the last judge, and his death appears to be the last event in the book, chronologically speaking. We are left with a dead judge, and a very incomplete rescue.

But there are four more chapters at the end of Judges! The previous passages have given us a bird's-eye view of things, only saying that the people "did evil in the eyes of the LORD" (3 v 7, 12; 4 v 1; 6 v 1; 10 v 6; 13 v 1). These chapters give us a ground-level, detailed view of what life was like in Israel during those times. These are case studies of the kind of spiritual condition God rescued them from.

That is why these final chapters barely mention the LORD. They are showing us what life was like when Israel was left to their own resources. And this view of humanity without God is so bleak that these passages are almost never preached on or even studied.

>> Read Judges 17 v 1-13

2. What is the approach of Micah and his mother in relating to God?

• v 3:

• v 4:

• v 5, 7-12:

• v 6:

• What is Micah's aim in all this (v 13)?

DICTIONARY

Consecrate (v 3): give something to be used to serve.
Shrine (v 5): a place where, it is believed, God is present, and can be accessed and worshiped.
Priest (v 5): men who were to perform sacrifices to God for the people, and teach the people about God.
Levite (v 9): a member of the tribe set apart to help the priests (priests were meant to be drawn from Aaron's family, among the tribe of Levi).

3. How is this different from the way God has told his people to relate to him?

>> Read Judges 18 v 1-31

4. What happens to Micah?

DICTIONARY

The captivity of the land (v 30): when the north of Israel was conquered by Assyria, in 722BC.
House of God (v 31): the tabernacle, the place where God had promised to dwell among his people.

• What is tragic about verse 24?

5. What is the Levite's career path (17 v 7-12; 18 v 18-21, 30-31)?

• What seems to be driving his decisions?

• What is tragic about the detail given about him in verse 30?

⤷ apply

6. Micah is essentially shaping God to fit his life and religion, rather than allowing God to shape them. How are we tempted to reshape God?

• How might we quietly copy his mother's approach to pleasing God (17 v 3-4)?

• How might we quietly copy the Levite's approach to ministry?

⊡ getting personal

Micah said of his religion: "What else do I have?" Centuries later, Peter said to Jesus: *Where else can we go?* (John 6 v 68).

You are a worshiper. The question is: Who or what do you look to for ultimate meaning, purpose, and blessing? So, is Jesus the one thing you cannot do without in life? What are the things which could easily take his rightful place in your heart?

⊕ investigate

This "appendix" to the book is in two parts: chapters 17 – 18 and chapters 19 – 21. A substantial part of both revolve around a Levite.

◑ Read Judges 19 v 1-30

7. This is horrific. How is the woman treated badly by:
   • the Levite?

DICTIONARY
Prevailed upon (v 4): convinced. **Alien (v 12):** foreign, non-Israelite.

   • her father?

   • the host?

   • the group of Gibeonite men?

⊡ explore more

optional

◑ Read Genesis 19 v 1-11, 24-28

What are the similarities between events in Sodom and in Gibeah? What happens to Sodom?

Sodom is the great Old Testament example of rebellion against God that rightly brings upon itself the judgment of God.

Gibeah is Israel's "showcase" here. So what does the similarity between Sodom and Gibeah tell us about:
   • *what Israel is like?*
   • *what Israel deserves?*

▶ Read Judges 20 v 1-17

8. How is the Levite's account an edited version of what really happened?

Understandably, Israel demands that the tribe of Benjamin hand over the criminals (v 12-13). Benjamin puts community and racial ties above the demands of justice, and refuses (v 13). Both sides muster their armies. The stage is set for civil war...

▶ Read Judges 20 v 18-48

The Benjamites lived in the hills, which favored a defending force. Twice, they defeat the far larger Israelite army. But eventually, God gives the rest of Israel victory (v 35-47).

9. What do the men of Israel do next (v 48)?

▶ Read Judges 21 v 1-25

Israel have now created a problem for themselves. They have sworn not to give any of their women in marriage to Benjamite men (v 1); and they have killed all the Benjamite women (20 v 48). They have effectively exterminated a whole tribe.

10. How do they solve the problem?

• v 5-14:

• v 15-23:

• Remember, all this started when a woman was raped and murdered. How are Israel's actions here desperately ironic?

⤷ apply

Bitterness always flowers into vindictiveness. On a tribal or national level, it looks like Judges 20 – 21. On a personal level, it looks less extreme, but is still destructive. And the only way to avoid bitterness and resentment is to practice forgiveness.

11. How can we do this?

• Luke 17 v 3-6:

• Matthew 18 v 21-35:

• Mark 11 v 25:

12. How is Judges 21 v 25 a good summary both of the book, and of the central problem of humanity?

• How does the book of Judges leave us aching for King Jesus?

⊡ getting personal

What is the single most helpful or striking truth that you have learned in your study of the book of Judges?

What difference is that truth making to your love of Jesus? Your obedience to God? Your attitude towards others?

⊡ pray

Spend time **confessing** to the Lord times when you have lived as though you have no King, either by reshaping God to suit your needs, or by ignoring him altogether.

Thank God that, despite our sin, he sent Jesus both to rescue us from ourselves and his anger, and to rule us perfectly and eternally.

Ask God to enable you to forgive as he has forgiven you, instead of living in bitterness and vindictiveness. If you're happy to, share as a group particular people you need to forgive, and pray for one another.

Judges: Leader's Guide

INTRODUCTION

Leading a Bible study can be a bit like herding cats—everyone has a different idea of what the passage could be about, and a different line of enquiry that they want to pursue. But a good group leader is more than someone who just referees this kind of discussion. You will want to:

• correctly understand and handle the Bible passage. But also…

• encourage and train the people in your group to do this for themselves. Don't fall into the trap of spoon-feeding people by simply passing on the information in the Leader's Guide. Then…

• make sure that no Bible study is finished without everyone knowing how the passage is relevant for them. What changes do you all need to make in the light of the things you have been learning? And finally…

• encourage the group to turn all that has been learned and discussed into prayer.

Your Bible-study group is unique, and you are likely to know better than anyone the capabilities, backgrounds and circumstances of the people you are leading. That's why we've designed these guides with a number of optional features. If they're a quiet bunch, you might want to spend longer on talkabout. If your time is limited, you can choose to skip explore more, or get people to look at these questions at home. Can't get enough of Bible study? Well, some studies have optional extra homework projects. As leader, you can adapt and select the material to the needs of your particular group.

So what's in the Leader's Guide?
The main thing that this Leader's Guide will help you to do is to understand the major teaching points in the passage you are studying, and how to apply them. As well as guidance on the questions, the Leader's Guide for each session contains the following important sections:

THE BIG IDEA

One or two key sentences will give you the main point of the session. This is what you should be aiming to have fixed in people's minds as they leave the Bible study. And it's the point you need to head back towards when the discussion goes off at a tangent.

SUMMARY

An overview of the passage, including plenty of useful historical background information.

OPTIONAL EXTRA

Usually this is an introductory activity that ties in with the main theme of the Bible study, and is designed to "break the ice" at the beginning of a session. Or it may be a "homework project" that people can tackle during the week.

So let's take a look at the various different features of a Good Book Guide:

⊕ talkabout

Each session kicks off with a discussion question, based on the group's opinions or experiences. It's designed to get people talking and thinking in a general way about the main subject of the Bible study.

⊍ investigate

The first thing you and your group need to know is what the Bible passage is about, which is the purpose of these questions. But watch out—people may come up with answers based on their experiences or teaching they have heard in the past, without referring to the passage at all. It's amazing how often we can get through a Bible study without actually looking at the Bible! If you're stuck for an answer, the Leader's Guide contains guidance on questions. These are the answers to direct your group to. This information isn't meant to be read out to people—ideally, you want them to discover these answers from the Bible for themselves. Sometimes there are optional follow-up questions (see ☑ in guidance on questions) to help you help your group get to the answer.

⊡ explore more

These questions generally point people to other relevant parts of the Bible. They are useful for helping your group to see how the passage fits into the "big picture" of the whole Bible. These sections are OPTIONAL—only use them if you have time. Remember that it's better to finish in good time having really grasped one big thing from the passage, than to try and cram everything in.

⊟ apply

We want to encourage you to spend more time working at application—too often, it is simply tacked on at the end. In the Good Book Guides, apply sections are mixed in with the investigate sections of the study. We hope that people will realize that application is not just an optional extra, but rather, the whole purpose of studying the

Bible. We do Bible study so that our lives can be changed by what we hear from God's word. If you skip the application, the Bible study hasn't achieved its purpose.

These questions draw out practical lessons that we can all learn from the Bible passage. You can review what has been learned so far, and think about practical differences that this should make in our churches and our lives. The group gets the opportunity to talk about what they personally have learned.

⊡ getting personal

These can be done at home, but it is well worth allowing a few moments of quiet reflection during the study for each person to think and pray about specific changes they need to make in their own lives. Why not have a time for reporting back at the beginning of the following session, so that everyone can be encouraged and challenged by one another to make application a priority?

⊞ pray

In Acts 4 v 25-30 the first Christians quoted Psalm 2 as they prayed in response to the persecution of the apostles by the Jewish religious leaders. Today however, it's not as common for Christians to base prayers on the truths of God's word as it once was. As a result, our prayers tend to be weak, superficial and self-centered rather than bold, visionary and God-centered.

The prayer section is based on what has been learned from the Bible passage. How different our prayer times would be if we were genuinely responding to what God has said to us through his word.

Some Hints for Leaders

Judges is not an easy book to read, nor to lead a group through! Here are a few pointers about how you and your Bible-study group can get the most out of these studies.

A BOOK ABOUT GOD

In Judges, God's people and even their leaders (the judges) are often dysfunctional and flawed. They do many appalling things, and we are led to ask: "Why on earth is *this* story in the *Bible?*" The answer is important—the Bible is not a book of virtues, of inspirational stories or of moral examples. It is a historical account of what happened, rather than a fictional story about what should happen. And it is about the actions of the God of the world, who is full of justice, mercy and patience, and who works in and through people despite their weaknesses and resistance. At the end of each study, your overriding impression should not simply be how terrible the people were, but also how glorious God is.

A BOOK FOR US TODAY

As you'll see in Study One, Israel ended up living in the land God had promised them, *but* co-existing there with other nations, who worshiped false gods—idols. Society was a mixture of pagan and believing peoples. There are many parallels between that situation and ours today. Largely due to the failures of the church, believers in western societies find themselves living in a religiously pluralistic society. Christians work and live among a great variety of gods—not only those of other formal religions, but also the gods of wealth, celebrity, pleasure, ideology, achievement. Our era can also be characterized by the phrase: "Everyone did what was right in his own eyes" (21

v 25, ESV). So Judges has much to say to the individualism and paganism of our own day.

READ WITH HUMILITY

It is easy for us to feel condescending toward the actions of many of the people we meet in Judges. It's important not to assume that, if we had been alive at that time, we would have been so much more enlightened than everyone else. We must remember that these kind of horrors still explode into life in our own day, in countries we would not have predicted and involving people who we would never have guessed at; not to mention the horrors of our own civilization. So as you read, do so humbly. Our own inner natures and hearts are not fundamentally better than these people's were. Their flaws may be different, but they flow from the same rebellious hearts as our own.

STAY ON TRACK

There are 21 chapters in Judges, and only six studies in this guide! Your group will be on a helicopter ride through the book, taking in key events, truths and surprises, but not hiking through every verse. So it's important not to let your group get off the flight-path each study moves along—otherwise you'll never finish any of the studies in the time you have! It would also be extremely useful if your group members read the passages beforehand—do encourage them to do this.

JUDGES FOR YOU

You will find a far slower, more detailed walk through the book of Judges (as well as an appendix on the issue of "Holy War") in *Judges For You*, the companion resource to this *Good Book Guide* (see p 77).

1 Judges 1 v 1 – 3 v 6
A SHAKY START

THE BIG IDEA
God's people go wrong when we fail to trust God's promises, and so don't obey him fully. We need his grace.

SUMMARY
Judges begins by looking backwards, to the time of Joshua (1 v 1). He was Moses' God-chosen successor, under whom Israel entered the land God had promised to give them, trusting his promises and obeying him. He called the people to obey God as he gave them the land; and not to worship the gods of the people in the land. We need to measure what happens in Judges by the yardstick of the commands in Joshua.

Chapter 1 shows us the history of the next generation, after Joshua died (1 v 1). They are faithful, but flawed. The tribes take a large part of the land God has promised; but they fail fully to drive out their enemies, where those enemies seem stronger or making them work as forced labor seems more convenient. It is a failure to trust God, and so to obey him.

Whereas chapter one reads like a collection of Israel's press releases, the beginning of chapter 2 is God's verdict on the campaign. And where Israel said: "We can't," God says that they were in fact saying: "We won't"—they wouldn't trust or obey him fully. And the nations who are still in the land will now be "thorns," and their gods "a snare" (v 3). The scene for Judges is set.

2 v 6 – 3 v 6 introduces us to the repeated cycle of the book. The people rebel (v 11-13); God is angry (v 12) and hands people over to their enemies (v 14-15). When Israel are in distress (v 15), and groan (v 18), God raises up a leader, a "judge," to rescue them (v 16). Under the judge's rule, things are better, but when the judge dies, the cycle begins again (v 19)—but with worse sin, and (as we'll see) weaker and weaker "revivals."

The other major theme of Judges introduced here is the ongoing tension between the conditionality of God's promises—*If you disobey, you will be punished* (2 v 2-3)—and their unconditionality—"I will never break my covenant" (2 v 1). We will see God acting in both judgment and mercy. But how can he reconcile them? As Q8 and 9 show, it is only possible at the cross, where God both punishes sin and forgives sinners.

OPTIONAL EXTRA
Conduct a trust exercise. Blindfold someone, and once they cannot see, ask a couple of others to stand behind them, ready to catch them. Then tell the blindfolded person to allow themselves to fall backwards. It is not easy to do this! But if they trust you, they will obey you (and if they don't, they won't). The lesson is that true trust shows itself in how we act—just as it did when it came to Israel and God.

GUIDANCE ON QUESTIONS
1. Why do things go wrong in churches?
For many, many reasons (many of which we will see in the course of Judges). And there are no wrong answers at this stage, though don't let this answer become a list of things that are wrong with your church, or with

"that church down the road." In this study, we'll see that God's people go wrong when they don't trust God fully, so don't obey him fully, and worship other "gods" instead. This is the root of all our problems, personally and collectively. So you might like to return to this question at the end of the study.

2. [In Joshua 1 v 1-9 and 23 v 3-13] What does God command Israel to do, both in Joshua's time and after he has died?
- Be strong and courageous in obeying God (1 v 6-9).
- Keep being strong and careful in obeying God and taking possession of the land (23 v 5-6).
- Keep "holding fast to" the LORD ie: knowing and serving and loving him.
- **What must they *not* do?**
  - Associate with (ie: make alliances or deals with) other nations (23 v 7, 12).
  - Worship other gods (v 7).
  - Marry people from other nations (v 12).

3. [In 1 v 1-36] How well does Israel obey God's commands in: You could divide your group into pairs or threes and give each mini-group a couple of these verses to think about, then come back together and briefly share answers.

- **v 1-2?** Very well. They are willing to fight the Canaanites, trusting God to give them victory; they ask God for guidance as to how to go about it.

- **v 3 (note what God had said in v 2)?** A mixture. Judah obey God in preparing to fight for the land God had promised them; but they ask another tribe, Simeon, to come and help them. God hadn't said anything about Simeon! Judah obey God, but not fully.

- **v 4-11?** Very well. Judah attack, and God gives victory, and they defeat the enemy

king, and then continue to take the land that God promised to give them.

- **v 19-21?** Not great. Despite the LORD being with Judah, they don't take the plains, because the people there have iron chariots. Benjamin don't take Jerusalem, and end up living there alongside the Jebusites (disobeying Joshua 23 v 7).

- **v 22-26?** Not well at all. Joseph attack Bethel, and God is with them, but then instead of fighting and winning, they make a deal with a Canaanite (v 23-25), who ends up living in Luz, within the land that God had promised his people. They disobey God's command not to make alliances with their enemies (Josh 23 v 12).

- **27-33?** Not well at all. Now, the list is more about where the tribes failed to drive out the Canaanites, rather than a list of where they succeeded. And even where Israel are, in their own strength, superior to the enemy, instead of driving them out they use them as forced labor.

- **v 34-36?** Really badly. The tribe of Dan are "confined … to the hill country" (v 34)— the Amorites are clearly dominant in this area of the land. Later, Joseph become stronger but do not drive them out (v 35). What matters in the end is not the boundaries of the land God promised to give Israel, but the border of their enemies, the Amorites (v 36).

4. Make a list of the reasons given (or hinted at) why the tribes of Israel failed to settle in all the land God had promised them, pushing the Canaanites out.
- v 19: Because the enemy were militarily stronger (they had iron chariots).
- v 25-26: Because they had become friendly and made a deal with a Canaanite.
- v 27: Because the Canaanites were

determined to hold onto the land.

- v 28, 30, 33, 35: Because they could use their enemies as forced labor.
- v 34-35: Because the enemy wouldn't let them take the land.

5. What examples of whole-hearted obedience do verses 12-16 show us?

- *Caleb:* (Along with Joshua, one of only two Israelites who left Egypt and did not disobey or disbelieve God in the desert, and so were allowed to enter the land—see Numbers 14 v 26-38). He believes Kiriath Sepher will be taken, and offers his daughter to the man who takes it. He wants for Acsah the life he chose for himself; one of faith and brave obedience.
- *Othniel:* He takes this town.
- *Acsah:* She wants to have her portion of the land (a field, v 14; springs, v 15).
- *The Kenites:* These are not Israelites, but distant relatives of Moses. Nevertheless, they go into the land "to live among the people." They must know God's promises, and they make them their own.

6. APPLY: How does this episode show us the difference between common sense and faithful obedience? Eg:

v 19: Common sense says: *They have iron chariots, and we do not. So there is no way we can win a battle with them. We will live in the hills, that's fine.* Faithful obedience says: *We are not strong enough to beat the men with iron chariots, but God is, and he's promised to do so. So we will attack, trusting God to keep his promises. Then we can enjoy all the land and blessing he's promised us.*

When we rely on ourselves, and base our walk with God on our own calculations instead of simply obeying, we find ourselves making decisions like the Judaites, instead of those like Caleb and Othniel. Sometimes

faithful obedience "agrees with" common sense; sometimes it is opposed to it. Wholehearted discipleship means following God's commands rather than our sense. You might like to ask the group to think of specific ways in which common sense and faithful obedience might prompt different actions in specific areas of your Christian lives.

7. [in 2 v 1-3] What is God's verdict on the same episode [ie: the campaign described in chapter 1]? "You have

disobeyed me" (v 2). Period. They have disobeyed through what they have done (making a covenant) and through what they have not done (breaking down the altars used to worship false gods). This disobedience is made more terrible by the reminder of what God has done for them already (v 1): rescuing them from Israel, and leading them into the land, keeping his promises.

Essentially, in chapter 1 the Israelites keep saying: *We could not....* God flatly contradicts this claim and answers: *You would not...*

8. What is the tension between what God had said before (v 1), and what he says now (v 3)?

- v 1: He has sworn to give the land to Israel, and that they will be his covenant people, enjoying the blessings of living with him in his land.
- v 3: He promises not to drive the Canaanites out of the land, so Israel will not enjoy the blessing of obeying God in his land, because the "people of this land" and their gods will be "thorns" and a "snare."

9. Read Romans 3 v 23-26; 2 Cor 5 v 21. How did God solve the dilemma, so

that he could be both just and forgiving to his people? It is only at the cross that we can see how God is able to resolve the tension. On the cross, our sin was given—imputed—to him, so that his righteousness could be imputed to us. On the cross, "God made him who had no sin to be sin for us, so that in him we might become the righteousness of God" (2 Corinthians 5 v 21). On the cross, God poured out his wrath on his people in the person of his Son. He satisfied both justice, because sin was punished, and loving faithfulness, since he is now able to accept and forgive us. Only through the cross can God be both "just and the justifier of the one who has faith in Jesus" (Romans 3 v 26, ESV). This is the only way the tension of Judges can be resolved; the only way that God can love us both conditionally and unconditionally.

- **What happens if we:**
  - **forget the conditionality of God's promises?** We will complacently give in to sin.
  - **forget the unconditionality of God's promises?** We will live under a burden of guilt and fear.

- **remember the conditionality and unconditionality of God's promises?** We are able to live forgiven, obedient lives while also living sinful, disobedient lives. We find the freedom to accept ourselves without being proud (because through the cross we are acceptable to God), and to challenge ourselves without being crushed (because through the cross we are acceptable to God).

10. What cycle in Israelite history do verses 10-21 summarize? See diagram below.

EXPLORE MORE
... Read Deuteronomy 6 v 4-9 and 20-25. What do we need to do to pass our faith on to the next generation?
- Love God whole-heartedly—to have these commandments on our hearts (v 5-6). We must not be hypocritical or inconsistent in our behavior (and must openly repent when we are).
- Apply and reflect on the gospel practically, not only academically. Verse 7 refers to the routine of daily life. Passing on truth is not about giving lectures, but about

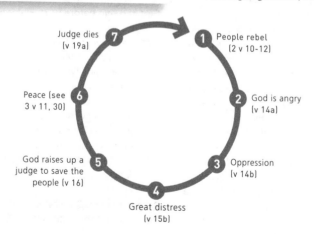

Judge dies (v 19a) — 7
Peace (see 3 v 11, 30) — 6
God raises up a judge to save the people (v 16) — 5
Great distress (v 15b) — 4
1 — People rebel (2 v 10-12)
2 — God is angry (v 14a)
3 — Oppression (v 14b)

showing how God relates to real, daily living, influencing our decisions, reactions, and priorities.

- We are to give regular, personal testimony to the difference God has made, and is making, to us (v 20-25). Our faith needs to clearly be a personal, living thing.

11. APPLY: how might we say: "I could not" but God says: "You would not," when it comes to:

- **forgiveness?** We say: *I just can't forgive him, or her, or myself.* But God commands us to forgive (Matthew 18 v 35). So we can do it, softening our hearts with the knowledge of God's grace to us, and acting as though the wrong hadn't happened. When we say we can't, we mean we won't give up our anger,

bitterness and "right" to get even.

- **telling the truth?** We say: *I just can't tell him the truth. It would destroy him / he would hate me.* God tells us to speak the truth, lovingly (Ephesians 4 v 15, 25). We can do it! When we say we can't, we mean we are not willing to risk being unpopular with someone, or upsetting them. At worst, we come first; at best, they come first; but we won't put God first.

- **being tempted?** We say: *I know this is wrong, but I just can't resist.* But God always gives us a way out (1 Corinthians 10 v 13). What we really mean is that we won't give up that sin, that we would like to commit it while excusing it.

2 Judges 3 v 7 – 5 v 31
OTHNIEL, EHUD, DEBORAH: EXPECT THE UNEXPECTED

THE BIG IDEA

God uses unlikely, marginalized, weak people of faith to win his victories and rescue his people.

SUMMARY

This study takes in the "cycles" of the first three "major" or "cyclical" judges (ie: the judges whose stories follow the cycle laid out in 2 v 10-19). Othniel (3 v 7-11) is a leader we would expect (see 1 v 13). Ehud (v 12-30) is unexpected, as he is a member of a less prominent tribe, and is left-handed—probably because his right hand is paralyzed. In his story, we see that God not

only works *around* someone's weakness, but he works *through* it, too—Ehud's left-handedness, something suspect in ancient societies, enabled him to kill Israel's enemy. In this, he foreshadows Christ, who achieved God's ultimate rescue at the moment of his greatest weakness, when he was derided and rejected by almost everyone.

Next follows Deborah (4 – 5), who is the greatest peacetime ruler, though she is a woman, and in that society would have again been an unexpected choice for God to work through. Yet despite being the leader, Deborah is not the warrior-rescuer. That role falls to Barak, a man whom Hebrews 11 v 32-34 tells us is an example of faith. There is some debate on how to read 4 v 9 (see Study Guide, p 16). I take the more positive view, which sees Barak as an exemplar of faith which listens to God's word; he acts courageously in response to God's promises; and doesn't act from a desire to gain honor.

Note: The life and work of Deborah is often raised in the debate over women's roles in church ministry (on several different "sides"!). It is worth remembering that women's roles are not the main concern of the writer of Judges! These chapters tell us what happened, not what should have happened (far less what ought to happen today). In fact, Deborah fits neither the "traditionalist" mold, where women are never in any type of leadership, in or outside the church; nor the "liberal" one, where women do everything a man does (it was Barak, not Deborah, who led Israel to war). There is not space in these notes to outline my position on women's ministry, but for more on my views, look at:
Judges For You, pages 54-58 (www.thegoodbook.com/judges-for-you)
Jesus, Justice and Gender Roles by Kathy Keller (ebook, available through Amazon)

OPTIONAL EXTRA

Split the group into pairs and give one of each pair a pencil, piece of paper and a card with the name of an object on it. That person must, using their "wrong" hand (left if they're right-handed, and vice versa), draw that object, and the other person in their pair tries to guess what it is. The first pair to do this successfully wins. If you want to, you can swap roles, and give out another object-card. This links to the idea that God not only uses us in areas where we think we are strong, but also where we know we are not—just as with Ehud.

GUIDANCE ON QUESTIONS

1. What stops people taking risks?
Many things—often entirely justifiable things. Sometimes circumstances; sometimes our own characters. You might like to ask the follow-up question: When is it a good idea to take a risk? This discussion does not need to be explicitly about matters of Christian living; the challenge of risk is one that often presents itself in business, parenting, and so on.
You could refer back to this question after Q4 and Q8, asking: How does Ehud/Barak take a risk? Why do they take that risk, do you think? How does this show us what living out our faith involves?

2. How do we see each stage of the "Judges cycle" in Othniel's story?
- v 7: Did evil—forgot God and served idols
- v 8a: God angry
- v 8b: God "sold them" to Cushan-Rishathaim, of Aram Naharaim
- v 9a: Cried out to the LORD
- v 9b-10: God raised up a Spirit-filled deliverer, Othniel, who saved them in battle
- v 11a: Peace
- v 11b: Othniel dies

3. What are the similarities between the Ehud episode [Judges 3 v 12-31], and the one featuring Othniel? The cycle is the same: doing evil (v 12); given over to an enemy (v 12-14); Israel cries out (v 15); God sends a judge (v 15); the judge leads Israel in battle and wins (v 28-30).

4. But how does Ehud's weakness enable him to defeat Israel's enemy?
First, he straps a sword to his right thigh, under his clothing (v 16). Right-handers carried their swords on their left, so this is where guards would search for hidden

weapons. Ehud's left-handedness means he can smuggle a weapon past Eglon's guards. Second, in v 19 Ehud approaches Eglon, who sends all his guards away. Because of his deformity, he appears to present no security threat. Therefore, he is able to be alone with Eglon, with a sword, and can kill him (v 20-22). Ehud's weakness means he is uniquely suited for the task of deliverance God has chosen him for!

5. Read Isaiah 53 v 2-6; Luke 23 v 33-39. How is Ehud a preview of the Lord Jesus?
Like Ehud, Jesus had "nothing in his appearance that we should desire him" (Isaiah 53 v 2-3)—people did not respect him. No-one understood that the dying Jesus was, like Ehud, God's plan to rescue his people. Like Ehud, Jesus did his saving work all alone. Jesus was, in this sense, a "left-handed" Rescuer. (Unlike Ehud, of course, Jesus used his weakness to offer forgiveness to his enemies, not to destroy them.)

- **Read 1 Corinthians 1 v 26-29. How is Ehud a preview of every follower of the Lord Jesus?** God did not choose his people based on our wisdom, influence or social status. In fact, the opposite—he chose those who are "foolish… weak… lowly" (v 27-28). He takes and saves and uses people who are at the margins of society—to show that salvation is from him, not from our human ability (v 29). Ehud was a weak man in the eyes of his society; but God chose him. It is the same with all of us as his people today (and if society does not view us as "left-handed" before we start following our "left-handed" Lord, it certainly will once we are followers of his!)

6. APPLY: How is knowing that we are "left-handed":

- **humbling?** We love to think there is something in us which contributes to our salvation, or to God choosing to work through us in some way. In truth, we are saved despite ourselves, and God works through us despite our weakness.

- **freeing?** We don't need to merit or earn salvation in any way, so we don't need to be anxious or lack assurance. And we don't need to be "good enough" in character or gifting for God to use us. Ehud shows us that God doesn't only work around our weaknesses; he uses the things we see as weaknesses to do his work. This is liberating.

- **How will remembering and rejoicing that we're we are "left-handed" change our Christian lives?**
  - We will not boast about ourselves (1 Corinthians 1 v 29).
  - We will praise God for saving us more and more, as we realize that we don't, and can't, deserve that salvation.
  - We will not think God can't save us, or that he can't use us. In fact, we will look for ways in which God might be wanting to use our weaknesses, as well as our God-given strengths. We will become bolder in taking risks to serve him.
  - We will not be surprised or discouraged if the world derides us, or our Savior.

7. How is Deborah [Judges 4 v 1-24] like Othniel and Ehud?
In the basic pattern: The Israelites did evil (v 1), so he "sold them" to the cruel oppression of Jabin, king of hazor, and his commander, Sisera (v 2-3); Israel cried for help (v 3); he provided Deborah (v 4—as a prophetess, she must already have had God's Spirit working in her); God gave victory in battle (v 15-16). *In the unexpected deliverer:* Though it was not unknown for women in ancient times

to be rulers and leaders, it was unusual. Worldly wisdom would not have looked for a women to lead Israel out of oppression.

- **How is she different?**
  - She does more than lead in battle (as Othniel and Ehud did)—she has a "courtroom" to which people bring their disputes (v 5).
  - In fact, she doesn't lead in battle at all! It is Barak, not Deborah, through whom God wins the battle (v 15-16). Alone of the judges, Deborah does not fight. The Ruler is not the Rescuer here.

8. On this second reading [see Study Guide page 16], how does Barak show us what real faith is? If your group struggle to pull out the three aspects of faith Barak shows, use the Extra Questions below.

- He recognizes that he needs God's guidance through his words, so he takes the prophetess Deborah with him (v 8). Faith is listening to God at every stage, in all circumstances.
- Sisera has 900 iron chariots, which could cut through foot-soldiers like hot knives through butter (v 13). 900 chariots will beat 10,000 men every time. Yet Barak still charges down the mountain (v 14). Why? He knows God has given him the victory. Faith is showing courage in the face of overwhelming odds; risking everything because you trust God's promises.
- Barak fights even though he knows "the honor will not be yours" (v 9): that he will neither have the honor of striking down Sisera (Jael does, v 21), nor lead Israel when there is peace (Deborah will). Faith is humble, and not honor-seeking (see the example of Jesus, Philippians 2 v 6-8).

⊗
- **What does Barak know he needs at all times (v 8)? Why would he want Deborah by his side?**
- **Why is it amazing that Barak charges down the mountain in v 14, given what we're told about his enemy in v 13? So why does he fight?**
- **What does Barak already know as he charges at the enemy (v 9)?**

9. How does Deborah's prophecy in verse 9 come true? See verse 17-22. Sisera flees to his ally, Heber (v 17), and is invited in by Heber's wife, Jael (v 18). But while he sleeps, she kills him with a tent peg (v 21). The honor of killing the man who has oppressed Israel (and abused women, see 5 v 28-30), goes to a woman, Jael, and not to Barak.

10. How does this chapter picture the battle between Barak's men and Sisera's forces (5 v 4-5, 19-22)? God marched with Barak's men (v 4), showing his power through nature (especially through pouring rain and earthquakes). As the "kings … fought" (v 19), nature fought under God's command on Israel's side (v 20), and the pouring rain meant the river flooded (v 21).

- **What does it tell us about why Israel won the battle?** Sisera wouldn't have ranged his chariots near a river if he was expecting rain—flooded ground renders chariots completely useless. It must have been the dry, not the wet, season—yet God caused it to rain so hard that the river flooded and "swept them away" (v 21).

EXPLORE MORE
How do you feel about what Jael did (4 v 18-22)? What was good? She struck down the main enemy of God's

people, and was brave (imagine if Sisera had happened to wake!) She showed that she was on God's side, wanting to be part of God's victory (she's a Kenite, not an Israelite—but, as we saw in Study One, 1 v 16, the Kenites had faith in Israel's God).

What was not good? Jael breaks two of the Ten Commandments—she implicitly lies to Sisera, and then murders him while he's asleep. While you could argue she is part of the battle, she has offered Sisera hospitality—in that culture there were strong rules of hospitality, and she breaks this code.

How does 5 v 24 describe her? Most blessed—in other words, her part in the story is approved of, though we have to remember that God often uses people to do what he wants without approving of all/any of their actions; and people often act commendably through faith, yet not all their decisions are individually commendable.

How would you square this with Jesus' command to love, pray for and bless our enemies in our personal relationships (Luke 6 v 27-28)? There is no easy answer, but since Jael is "blessed" by Scripture, and the same Scriptures recount Jesus telling us to treat our enemies very differently, it is an important question to ask! Take any suggestions, but if there are none go straight onto the next question...

How do the following passages show us how we should think about enemies: (If you need to save time, split into four groups, each taking a passage and reporting back.)

• **Revelation 11 v 15-18?** God's triumph over evil, and the fact that those who disobey him and mistreat/destroy people will one day face God's deserved anger, is good news, which we should welcome (though we tremble as we do so, knowing that but for the grace of God we would stand alongside them).

• **Romans 12 v 14, 19-20?** Coming

judgment frees us from the need to see, or right to bring, justice in this life. God is the one who judges those who do wrong (sometimes in this life, always in the next); so we are wrong to seek revenge now, and freed to get on with going out of our way to bless those who curse us (v 14, 20).

• **Acts 17 v 31?** We can be certain that justice will be done because God has proved it through raising the One who will judge from the dead.

• **Luke 23 v 34?** Because of the cross (where we see that God does judge sin), we can yearn for justice and pray for our enemies—as the Lord Jesus did as he was crucified. The death and resurrection of Christ fundamentally change our attitude toward our enemies.

11. APPLY: ... In what ways do [David and Maria] need to have each of the three aspects of faith that Barak did (see Q8)?

• God's word tells us to "make disciples of all nations" (Matt 28 v 18-20) and to take opportunities to share his gospel with others (Colossians 4 v 5-6). Faith for David and Maria will mean remembering God's word—taking it "with them" in their day.

• Faith acts courageously! They will need to ignore the thought that none of their co-workers/friends will likely come, and risk inviting them along, trusting that God can use them to do great things.

• They will need to remember not to seek their own honor or reputation, but be prepared to give it up in order to start up a conversation about the gospel.

• **Think about what might happen if they forget one of them.**

  • Forgetting God's word or forgetting to apply it to their day will mean they won't invite them, or even think of doing so.

- Not having courage, deciding that there's no point in inviting them because they probably will say no, will mean they won't invite their friends.
- Seeking their own honor/reputation means they'll either stay quiet, not wanting to risk friendships; or they'll invite them along for wrong reasons (eg: because they want to have the "honor" of being seen by their Christian friends to bring unbelievers to church).

12. APPLY: What happens when we have only a Judges-4 "historical" perspective on our lives, and forget to combine it with a Judges-5 "theological" perspective? We don't see God's hand at work in, through and around us. We forget God is involved; he becomes distant from us. We over-honor ourselves in our successes, and despair in our struggles. Maintaining a Judges-5 perspective—living our lives and ordering our memories not only "historically," but "theologically"—means we'll praise God for what we see him doing, trust him when we can't see how he's at work, and want to serve him each day. **Why is it easy to do this?** Our sinful nature wants to honor itself and worship something other than God; and we're often surrounded by those who reject the idea of a personal, loving God, who live only out of "Judges 4."

3

Judges 6 v 1 – 8 v 31

GIDEON: THE DANGERS OF SUCCESS

THE BIG IDEA

God works through and in our weakness, so that we see it is he who saves and gives success. So we mustn't misuse God-given success as an opportunity to seek honor and glory for ourselves.

SUMMARY

The life of Gideon teaches us two things:

(1) That it is God who saves, through unlikely people and in unlikely ways—and one reason he works like this is to teach his people that he is the One who gives salvation and success, not us. He removes any grounds for us boasting in our own goodness or strength. This is why he chooses Gideon, who does not consider himself leadership material (6 v 14-16) and is slow

to be assured of God's plans (v 36-40); and why he reduces Gideon's army from 32,000 to 300 (7 v 1-8)—"in order that Israel may not boast against me that her own strength has saved her" (v 2).

(2) That God's people are very bad at learning this lesson! After God gives him victory, Gideon feels that he should be honored, and avenges those who don't give him this respect (8 v 4-9, 13-17); and though he won't allow himself to be called a king (because God is Ruler, 8 v 23), he then lives like one, seeking honor for himself and his family (v 24-31). So the "lesson of the 300"—that God brings salvation and that God gives all "success," and that he deserves all the honor—is one we need to learn and keep re-learning today.

OPTIONAL EXTRA

Play the children's game "Top Trumps." The idea of this game is that the subject of the cards (eg: cars, fiction superheroes, etc) are rated against one another in different categories, and the fastest/strongest/ oldest etc wins. The point is that this is how life usually works; and this is how God deliberately *doesn't* work. He "wins" through using people's weaknesses, to show that it is he who gives victory.

GUIDANCE FOR QUESTIONS

1. What are the dangers of success?
You may want to talk about celebrities or politicians or more locally; and talk about success in secular life, or in our spiritual lives. Answers might include: complacency; dissatisfaction and despair; pride/arrogance; not knowing who your real friends are; forgetting what really matters in life; etc.

2. What is different in this cycle:

• **with the oppression (v 1-6)?** This is the worst yet—the Israelites are forced to leave their homes and "prepare shelters for themselves" in the inaccessible mountains (v 2). The Midianites were after economic exploitation, plundering crops (v 3). They "did not spare a living thing" (v 4)—the people were starving (v 5).

• **with how God responds to the Israelites crying out to God (v 7-10)?** When they "cried to the LORD" we expect God to raise up a deliverer, a judge (see 3:9, 15; 4 v 3-4, 6-7). Instead, "he sent them a prophet" (v 8). God's first response to the people's cry is not to send a savior, but a sermon! He reminds them of two things: what he has done (rescued them, freed them, given them a land—v 8-9), and what they have done (not listened to him, and worshiped other gods—v 10).

3. What does this suggest about the type of "crying" Israel is doing? They are not really sorry. They are regretful—they don't like being oppressed by Midian; but not repentant—they aren't sorry for disobeying God. They are upset about what their sin has caused—oppression—rather than about their sin itself. **Why do the people need a prophet before they have a rescuer?** Before they can appreciate the rescue that will come, the people need to understand why they need rescuing. The prophet comes and helps them to understand why they are in the trouble they are in. He wants them to understand where their idolatry—their sin—has led them.

4. When the angel of the LORD visits Gideon, how do their opinions differ on whether God has forgotten his people (v 13-14)? In response to the angel's opening assurance: "The LORD is with you" (v 12), Gideon suggests that he isn't (v 13)! His argument is: *God clearly isn't with us, because he has put us into Midian's hands instead of rescuing us as he did our ancestors.* The readers know God put them into the hands of Midian because he had *not* abandoned them, but was showing them the poverty of idolatry, so that they would return to him. God's point has already been made through his prophet (v 10): *I have not abandoned you, but you have abandoned me.* Now, when Gideon suggests they need an Egypt-style rescuer—another Moses—God says: *You are the salvation I am sending. You are my mighty warrior* (v 12).

• **How are both God and Gideon correct about Gideon's ability (v 12, 15)?** The angel calls Gideon a "mighty warrior" (v 12). Gideon objects that he is "the least in my family" (v 15)—he is the poorest member of the weakest clan of a insignificant Israelite tribe. "How can I save Israel?" he asks (v 15). Gideon is correct! He can't save Israel, on his own. But God is correct, too. If Gideon combines his own strength with his divine calling to this task, and trusts in God to work through him to do what alone he never could, then he can be a "mighty warrior."

EXPLORE MORE

Who speaks in v 12 and v 20? "The angel of the LORD."

Who speaks in v 14, 16, 18? What is strange about this? The LORD. This figure is both the angel *of* the LORD, and yet also *the* LORD? This is one of the mysteries of the OT.

How does Gideon react when he realizes who he has been speaking to (v 22)? He understands that he has seen the angel of the LORD/sovereign LORD "face to face." He thinks he's going to die (see the response of the LORD, in verse 23).

What does this tell us about who he has seen (see Exodus 33 v 20)? To look upon *God's* face is to die (Exodus 33 v 20). Gideon knows that, in seeing the angel of the LORD, he has seen God.

Who do you think this "angel" (literally "messenger"), who is both the LORD and not the LORD, is? There is good reason to see this figure as Christ, the Son. This event is an indication, deep in the OT, that the one God is multi-personal; a hint of the Trinity.

5. How does God command or enable Gideon to begin to deal with: • the enemy among God's people (v 25-32)? Within God's people—within Gideon's family—are an altar and pole for worshiping Canaanite gods. Before they can throw off the enemy around them, Israel needs to deal with the enemy among themselves—their idolatry. Gideon's first task as God's deliverer is to deal with idols, not circumstances.

• **the enemy around God's people (v 33-35)?** "The Spirit of the Lord came upon Gideon" (v 34). God does not call the equipped; he equips the called, through the gift of his Spirit. Thus strengthened, Gideon calls God's people together.

• **the enemy within Gideon (v 36-40)?** Gideon is struggling truly to believe God's word (v 36, 39). He seems worried that, if he gives himself utterly in the LORD's service, the LORD will let him down. God enables Gideon to deal with his unbelief through the famous signs of the fleeces (v 38, 40). The narrative doesn't make clear whether this was a good thing for Gideon to do, or not. But notice that Gideon is not looking for a sign so much as to understand who God is—is he sovereign over the forces of nature? Is he powerful? We have God's indwelling Spirit, the Bible, baptism and communion, and the church to enable us to know this—so we don't need to "lay fleeces." But we do learn that God responds to requests to expel unbelief and build up faith; just as Jesus responded to a man's plea of: "I do believe; help me overcome my unbelief!" (Mark 9 v 24).

6. APPLY: How is the answer to the 2nd part of Q4 a picture of what it means to be a Christian? In ourselves, and by our abilities, we cannot do anything about our enemies of oppression and idolatry—we are sinners. But, called by God and trusting in his power and forgiveness, we find that God uses us and our abilities to do what we never could have done on our own.

🗨

• **What happens when we forget one "side"?** If we forget our sinfulness, we become over-confident, unloving, bad listeners, judgmental, undisciplined in prayer. If we forget our acceptance and beloved-ness, we become anxious, guilty, despairing, and so on.

- **How are the answers to Q5 a picture of what it means to live as a Christian?** It is helpful to talk about the three parts of Q5 in reverse. A Christian is someone:
  - who informs their beliefs by the revealed character of God; who knows who God is by humbly listening to his self-revelation in his word; and who asks God to overcome their natural unbelief.
  - who relies on God's Spirit, working alongside God's people, to oppose those things which are opposed to God and his people in this world.
  - who is uncompromising and clear about the Lord's call on every aspect of their lives, loves and worship, and who clears out idols and worships God.

☒

- **What happens when we forget one aspect?**
  - We have a deficient view of who God is; or we live rightly externally, but don't truly trust God (which will be seen in inaction where action is risky).
  - We rely on ourselves; or "go it alone"; or cave in to worldly opposition
  - We worship God alongside other things; some aspects of our lives are taken up in pursuit of, and therefore ruled by, money or power or something else.

7. What does God do to Gideon's army? He reduces it from 32,000 to 10,000 (7 v 3), and then to 300 (v 4-8).

- **What lesson does God want to teach him, and Israel (v 2)?** "In order that Israel may not boast against me that her

own strength has saved her." God wants Gideon and Israel to praise him for this victory, not themselves. Human nature is such that, if there is the tiniest opportunity to boast in our own work, we will—we will see ourselves as our own saviors. But this is to take glory that God deserves and give it to ourselves. By reducing the army to 300, God is helping Israel to say: *We could not possibly have done this ourselves. It was all God's doing.*

8. How does God reassure Gideon (v 8b-15)? God reaffirms that he will give Gideon victory (v 9), then tells him to go to the enemy camp and listen to their conversations (v 9-11). There, Gideon hears about a soldier's dream (v 13), and his friend interpreting it as a sign that God has given them into Gideon's hands (v 14). So God reassures Gideon through his word (v 9b); through the words of others (v 13-14); and through circumstances (he took Gideon to just the right place, at the right time).

- **How does Gideon's response show that he has received assurance?** v 15: he worships and confidently obeys God.

9. How should the manner of the victory (v 16-23) help Gideon and Israel to trust in God, and not boast in themselves? The battle is won without Gideon or his men doing any actual fighting! They hold their positions (v 21), and the Midianites flee, killing each other (v 22-23). God gives them a victory without them doing anything.

10. Neither Gideon nor Israel has learned "the lesson of the triumph of the 300." How do we see that here?
- **Ephraim:** The tribe of Ephraim are annoyed they missed out on the glory of being part of the victory (v 1). But the 300

did not gain honor for themselves; all that went to God, anyway. Ephraim has not realized who won the victory, nor who should get the praise.

- **The inhabitants of Succoth and Peniel:** These Israelites refuse to help Gideon (8 v 6, 8), because Gideon has not yet destroyed the kings of Midian; they know that if he can't, the Midianites will regroup, return, and destroy any towns who helped Gideon. They haven't learned to trust God to keep his promises, however against-the-odds they are.

- **Gideon:** His dealings with Succoth and Peniel (v 6-9, 16-17) show that he wants respect and honor for his victory. He does not say to them, when they refuse to help him: *I know it's hard to believe we can beat them. But it's God who wins for us, so don't trust my strength, trust his.* He says: *You dare to doubt me? I'll show you my power—you'll learn to respect me.*

11. But how do Gideon's actions then not match up with his words [in 8 v 24-31]?

- v 24-26: He asks for financial reward, which is a king-like thing to do (notice that he doesn't disagree with their assessment in verse 22 that "you have saved us").
- v 27: Gideon makes an ephod (which was worn by the high priest in the tabernacle, the tent where God was present among his people, and which had on its front two stone that were used to guide the people according to God's will). He's pointing towards himself, and his town, as where God can be met and where his guidance should be sought. He leads the people to worship him/his ephod, rather than God .
- v 29-31: He takes many wives and concubines (second-class wives), which is a way kings proved their power. His son by

his concubine is named "Abimelech" (v 31), meaning "My father is king."

12. APPLY: What do we learn from Gideon about the dangers of God-given success? Success can easily cause us to forget God's grace, because our hearts are desperate to believe that we can save ourselves. God-given victory can easily be used to confirm the belief that, in fact, we have earned blessing ourselves, and should receive the praise and glory for that success.

- **How is it possible to make the same mistakes today?** One example is a man who works very hard at his job because he needs to prove himself through financial success. What is the worst thing that can happen to him? The obvious answer is: *career failure.* True, someone who is basing their happiness and identity on their work will be devastated by career failure. But at least, through the failure, he may stop idolizing career advancement. He may realize that status and money could never fulfill him. No, the worst thing that can happen to him is career success. Success will only confirm his belief that he can fulfill himself and control his own life. He will be more a slave to success and money than if he failed. He will feel proud and superior to others. He will expect deference and "bowing and scraping" from others.

Or imagine someone in a position of leadership in their church. It is easy to end up doing ministry not to serve and honor God, but to win influence and honor for ourselves. Of course, Gideon-like, we still say that God is King; but we want people to look to us for guidance, for answers, and for salvation. We need to be needed. We make an ephod and wear it ourselves.

13. APPLY: How does the "Gideon episode" show us that God is great?

- He shows his people their disobedience; yet he still saves them.
- He takes weak, scared, doubting people and uses them mightily.
- He reassures his people through his word, through others, and through circumstances.
- He wins victories which are impossible, humanly-speaking.

Judges 8 v 32 – 12 v 15

4 ABIMELECH & JEPHTHAH: DARK TIMES

THE BIG IDEA

God's people's greatest problem is us: our own failings, and our own misunderstandings of God. Yet God both graciously judges sin and saves his people.

SUMMARY

In Abimelech and Jephthah, we continue to see how the book of Judges is not just circular, but is a downward spiral. Abimelech is not even a "judge": he comes to power through brute, murderous force, rather than being called by God. In fact, the next judges (Tola and Jair) appear to have rescued Israel from Israel—from the reign of Abimelech. What is noticeable about Judges 9 is that God appears absent; but in two comments by the narrator (v 23-24, v 56-57) we see that, in fact, God is judging sin unseen, in his own time, and through allowing people to experience the consequences of their sin.

Jephthah is a judge, and again we see the all-too-familiar cycle. What is tragic is how little Jephthah himself appears to know God. He does seem to believe that God is a God of grace, who keeps his promises and rescues his people. In trying to "earn" God's blessing, Jephthah ends up murdering his own daughter; and then goes on to murder many of his own countrymen. For the first time, there is no "peace" in the cycle.

This is a dark time in Israel's history: it contains many "negative lessons" for God's people today. It also reminds us just how gracious God is, to work through such flawed individuals to save such a flawed people.

OPTIONAL EXTRA

To introduce the topic of leadership, print some pictures of famous leaders (good and bad) from the past. (It is probably best to avoid recent leaders in your own country, to avoid unnecessary division in your group!) Ask people to order them in terms of how good/bad they were; and then in terms of how much influence they had on the people they led, for good or ill.

GUIDANCE FOR QUESTIONS

1. What makes for bad leadership? There are no "wrong answers" (your group may choose to focus on leadership of nations, or businesses, schools, families, churches, etc). Selfishness—using leadership for your own ends, to satisfy your own desire for security, or respect, or wealth, or control—is usually at the root of bad leadership. In this study, we'll see two leaders of Israel who both made serious mistakes as leaders, and we'll see why. You could return to this question at the end of the study, asking what Abimelech- and Jepththah-like mistakes would look like in the leadership of a nation; of a church; and in a home (ie: husband and parents).

2. [In Judges 8 v 33 – 10 v 5] How is Abimelech different from the judges who have come before his time?

- There is no "cycle." The Israelites, on Gideon/Jerub-Baal's death, forget God and worship an idol (8 v 33-34). But God does not appear to hand them over to enemies, and he does not raise up a judge.
- Abimelech rises to lead not through God's call, but because he is a son of Gideon and promises strong rule (9 v 1-2).
- He is recognized as leader not because he will throw off any oppressor, but because he has butchered his own family (v 4-6). And he governs without any word from the LORD to guide him, but simply through a naked exercise of power.
- He is considerably more violent than any of the previous judges (v 5, 39-49).

So Abimelech is not really a judge at all! He is more of an oppressor than he is a deliverer. And he comes to power using the wealth of an idol (9 v 4) instead of the Spirit-given power of God.

3. What brings Abimelech down:

- **9 v 23:** "God sent an evil spirit" to disturb relations between Abimelech (who as we've seen is willing to do anything for power) and the people of Shechem (who, 9 v 1-2 shows, are happy to switch loyalties for their own ends). What follows is an outworking of this spirit being sent.

- **v 26-29:** Another man like Abimelech moves into Shechem. He uses the same arguments as Abimelech, and the Shechemites switch allegiance. Abimelech's power base has gone.

- **v 50-55:** Advancing on the town of Thebez to kill its inhabitants, a woman drops a millstone—a very heavy, circular stone used for grinding corn—on Abimelech's head. Dying, but mindful of his reputation, he has his servant kill him.

- **v 56-57:** The narrator makes clear that working through all these events was God, who was ensuring that Abimelech paid for his massacre, and Shechem paid for their idol-worship and disloyalty.

- **If you had been an Israelite at the time, which of these could you have seen?** Only the second and third! A history book would not record that these things happened as a result of God sending a spirit to cause division, in judgment. **Which would you not have known about?** The sending of the spirit, and the verdict that this was God's judgment. To the naked eye, this simply looks like falling-out between Abimelech and Shechem, a lot of blood spilt, and a lucky throw by a woman in Thebez.

4. How does ch 9 show us the answer to that question [of who Tola saved Israel from]? Israel need saving from Abimelech, and Shechem—in other words, Israel need saving from Israel! They need to be rescued from the blood-letting that has occurred because they are worshiping idols and choosing the wrong leaders.

- **What does it tell us is the greatest problem God's people have?** Ourselves. Our failings and flaws, our divisions and strife. We need rescuing not from problems "out there," but those which are "in here." Our forgetting God and loving idols may not cause such horrific crimes as those of Abimelech and Shechem did—but they are the root cause of our problems. Always before, God has raised up a judge to deliver people from an external oppressor—here, it appears to be from the results of the mistakes of God's people. No non-Israelites were required to bring Israel to its knees. They did it themselves.

5. APPLY: Paul says in Rom 1 v 18: "The wrath of God is being revealed from heaven against all the godlessness and wickedness of men who suppress the truth by their wickedness." What does the story of Abimelech show us about God's present judgment? Three things:

- *It comes unseen.* The people could not have seen the spirit God sent to use the evil in Shechemite hearts for his just purposes. In our own day, we have no divinely-inspired narrator to lift the curtain to tell us where, when and how God is judging people. We know it is happening; but we can't point to any an event and say: *God is judging you for this particular sin you have committed.* This is very important: we must *never* say: *This storm happened to this city because of this sin.*

- *It comes after a wait.* Three years passed between Jotham warning of judgment and judgment coming (v 22-23), during which Abimelech ruled, his sin appearing to have paid off. The wait is covered in a single verse (v 22). To Jotham, those three years must have seemed considerably longer! He had to learn patience and trust.

- *It comes through the outworking of human sin.* Shechem was destroyed because of its disloyalty. Its greatest sin was its downfall. Abimelech was destroyed because of his desire to maintain his position at any human cost. He had no

need to attack Thebez. His greatest sin was also his downfall. God in his judgment uses sinfulness, the tools of human rebellion, against those who rebel.

- **How is this encouraging to us today?** Romans 1 v 18 is true! God is at work in this world, in salvation but also in judgment, and evil does not go unpunished. In general terms, God pays people what they deserve, in one way or another. This once more reminds us that we don't need to, and must not, seek vengeance for ourselves (see Study Two). God is powerful and just, and at work, both in present and future judgment.

6. How does God respond [to Israel crying out] (10 v 11-14)? He points out that he has saved them many times before (v 11-12); yet Israel has, once again, been unfaithful to him and served false gods (v 13); and therefore "I will no longer save you." Instead, they should look for salvation from the gods they've chosen to worship. **What does he want the people to realize in verse 14, do you think?** That they cannot have both him and their idols. God demands exclusive loyalty and love from his people. They cannot truly worship the LORD if they worship idols alongside him. Here, God is saying: *You have chosen to love gods other than me. So now you need to rely on them to rescue you.* And they can't, of course! The people need to realize that ultimately, an idol is a non-god, who cannot save. And they need to realize that true, heart-felt "crying out to the LORD" involves more than just words—it involves turning back to him as the one true God.

- **How does verse 16 show that Israel have understood?** At last, they get rid of the "foreign gods," who can't save them (which shows that in v 11, as they cried out to God, they had no intention of stopping their idolatry). In v 16, they are finally pledging exclusive allegiance to the LORD as their God, and serving him. They have understood they cannot have both-and—both asking God for help, and keeping idols as an insurance policy. It is either-or—either serve idols and see if they save, or serve God and be saved by him.

⊻

- **How can we make the same mistake, saying the right things to God and expecting him to save us, but keeping hold of idols as "insurance"?**

7. How does the Gileadites' treatment of Jephthah, God's chosen judge, mirror their treatment of God? The Gileadite leaders have shunned Jephthah, excluding him from their society (11 v 2-3); but when they are in trouble they turn to him (v 4-6). They want him to win a battle for them as commander, but they don't want him to be their "head," their leader. This is just how they have treated God (10 v 6, 9-10). Jephthah, like God, points out that they have no right to ask for his help, because of how they have treated him (11 v 7; 10 v 11-14). They respond by asking him for help again, with more humility, and now agreeing that their rescuer will also be their ruler (11 v 8, 10)—just as they had finally humbly begged God for rescue, and made him their God (10 v 15-16).

⊻

- **Jesus is God's ultimate "judge." How does the parallel treatment of God and Jephthah help us to see the link between our treatment of Jesus and our treatment of God?** The way we treat God's leader is a reflection of

how we are truly treating God. The way people today treat Jesus is the way they are, in fact, treating God. You cannot respect God, or truly repent, without acknowledging the right of Jesus to rule. And you cannot have Jesus' rescue without accepting his rule. Many people say they worship God or respect God or experience God, but reject Jesus as God's ultimate Judge. But since the way we treat Jesus is the way we are treating God, this shows that in fact they are not really worshiping, respecting or experiencing the true God.

- **How is this helpful for us in talking to unbelieving friends about God?**

EXPLORE MORE

How does Jephthah respond to the king of Ammon's claim that part of Israel's land used to belong to the Ammonites:

- **in 11 v 15-22?** This is a historical argument: the Ammonites did not live in the disputed land, but the Amorites (a similarly named but different nation!) did (v 19). They attacked Israel (v 20); Israel won the battle, so won the land by right of conquest (v 21). Historically speaking, the land was never the Ammonites', and was won fairly by Israel from the Amorites.
- **in v 23-24?** A theological argument. He uses an assumption held by all the people of that time; a nation's god gave them their land. The LORD (Israel's God) had given Israel this land, by giving them victory over the Amorites (v 23), just as the Ammonites would have it if Chemosh (their god) gave them victory (v 24).
- **in verses 25-27?** A legal precedent. The king of Moab (v 25) and the Ammonites' ancestors (v 26) had not disputed Israel's right to this land. Why should the current king of the Ammonites, centuries later?

How does the king of Ammon respond (v 28)? He "paid no attention"—he neither replies nor retreats.

Read 1 Peter 2 v 21-25. How are Jephthah and Jesus examples of the way we should respond to unfair accusations? We must seek to speak peacefully rather than assuming there must be conflict. We must tell the truth calmly and rationally. We must not retaliate or make threats. We must trust the one who judges justly (Judges 11 v 27; 1 Peter 2 v 23). And we must remember that, even if we do all that, we will very probably still be misunderstood, ignored, or mocked.

8. What happens instead [of there being peace], and why? • within Jephthah's family (11 v 30-31, 34-39): Jephthah vows to the LORD that if he gives him victory, he will offer as a sacrifice the first thing that leaves his house on his return (v 30-31). The first thing out of the door is his only child, his daughter (v 34). He "did to her as he had vowed" (v 39). **Note:** we will look into why this horrific thing happened in Q9.

- **within the people of Israel (12 v 1-6):** The men of Ephraim threaten Jephthah's life (12 v 1). He justifies his position (v 2-3), and, without waiting for a response, goes on the offensive (v 4). 42,000 members of God's people die at the hands of God's people (v 6). The narrator, unsurprisingly, does not record in verse 7 that there was "peace" during Jephthah's rule.

9. Why do you think Jephthah made the vow in the first place? God does not want human sacrifice (Deuteronomy 12 v 31). Yet Jephthah promises human sacrifice—if he'd meant an animal, he'd have used a neuter form of the noun "whatever" (Judges 11 v 31). He obviously expected it to be a

servant—not his only child. So why? The text isn't explicit, but here are two suggestions:

- He had been deeply desensitized to violence by his treatment by the other Gileadites, and by the cruelty of the pagan cultures around him—where child sacrifice was common. He had let the beliefs of the world around him come in and live alongside his right beliefs.
- Jephthah had a pagan attitude to God—he did not truly believe God is a God of grace, who keeps his promises. Human sacrifice was how you could buy the favor of a pagan god. Jephthah seems to have believed that he needed to offer something to God in order for God to have compassion and rescue his people.

- **Why do you think he kept the vow in such a horrific way?** When Jephthah realizes his foolish vow has trapped him (v 35), he should just confess its foolishness, ask for forgiveness, break the vow and save his daughter. He does none of those things—he makes the sacrifice. Again, he doesn't understand who God is—he seems to believe that God will strike him down if he doesn't keep his end of "the deal." So the tragedy is that, because Jephthah misunderstood God, he failed to realize that God had already decided to have compassion (10 v 16), and had already empowered Jephthah to be his agent of rescue (11 v 29).

10. APPLY: What are the lessons for us from Jephthah's family tragedy?
- Clearly, it teaches us to be careful with our words. Once said, they cannot be unsaid. We need to pray, like the writer of Psalm 141, that God would "set a guard over my mouth" (Psalm 141 v 3).
- It reminds us that God can write straight with crooked pencils. We must beware mistaking God's work through us for

evidence that God has finished his work in us. Just because we are good speakers, leaders, or teachers, and just because God is using us, does not mean our hearts are pleasing to him.

But there are two deeper lessons, too:

- We are always far more affected by our culture than by the Bible—and we are far more affected by our culture than we think. It is easy for us to see how Jephthah ignored what the Scriptures he had (the first five books of our Bible) told him about who God is, and how sacred human life is; how, instead, he listened to pagan culture about God and about life. But surely many people at other times and places would be astounded at (for example) how much money Christians in western culture spend on themselves. Jephthah makes us look at ourselves and ask: *What enormous blind spots do I have?* If we really want to know the answer to that question, we will be regular and humble Bible-readers.

- God's people struggle to believe in a God of grace. In the Garden of Eden, the first lie of the serpent was to make humans disbelieve that God had their best interests in mind (Genesis 3 v 1-5). Since then, we have always felt we had to control God, to pay God and deserve God; that we cannot simply trust God to love and bless us. It is worth asking: What ways would I live differently—more radically or restfully—if I really believed God was completely committed to me to love me and bless me and work what is best for me?

11. APPLY: What are the lessons for us from Ephraim's tragedy? We need to be the opposite of both Ephraim and Jephthah. Ephraim (as we saw in Gideon's day) are hungry for honor, and angry when they feel "left out." Jephthah is impatient and vengeful, and his reactions are massively out of proportion. One side makes threats (12 v 2); the other is violent (v 4-6).

The lessons are to "be quick to listen, slow to speak and slow to become angry, for man's anger does not bring about the righteous life that God desires" (James 1 v 19-20). We need to remember to live like this with our Christian brothers and sisters (even, and especially, when they aren't remembering to). The outcome of our failures to love fellow Christians when they are disagreeing or being unfair to us may not be a massacre, but it can be refusing to forgive, gossiping, seeking some kind of revenge, shunning them in some way, and so on. If we learned the lessons of the tragedy of Ephraim, our communities would be far less divided and far more loving.

12. APPLY: How do these two dark episodes in Israel's history show us how wonderful God is?

The darker God's people are seen to be, the brighter God's grace shines out! Ask people to pick out a verse showing how wonderful our God is, and to say why it's wonderful that he is like this today. For example:

- 10 v 11-13: Instead of ignoring us when we try to worship God and idols, God gently points out what we are doing and challenges us to serve him alone.

- v 16: God has compassion on his people. He feels our misery, self-inflicted though it is, and acts to save us.

- 11 v 29: God gives his Spirit to his chosen rescuer.

- v 32: God gives his (deeply flawed) judge victory over his people's enemies.

- Of course, the more we realize how deeply sinful we are, the more we are able to appreciate the wonder of God's love in sending our perfect Savior, the Lord Jesus.

5 Judges 13 – 16

SAMSON: A SHADOW IN THE DARKNESS

THE BIG IDEA

The greatest danger to the church is becoming just the same as the surrounding culture, as Samson's life shows us. The only hope for the church is Jesus' rescuing death, as Samson's own death shows us.

SUMMARY

The life of Samson is exciting; full of sex, violence, death and power. But it is also disturbing and disappointing. He is the last judge, and his miraculous birth prepares us for a wonderful, powerful deliverer.

Instead, we find by far the most flawed character in the book; a violent, impulsive, sex-driven, ungodly, complacent man. He uses his Spirit-given strength selfishly, to extricate himself from the trouble his weaknesses get him into. He is an individual picture of the state of Israel as a whole—virtually indistinguishable from the pagan Philistines, and quite happy to exist under their rule instead of under God's (15 v 9-13).

Yet Hebrews 11 v 32-34 lists Samson as a hero of faith. This must be referring to his death, where at last he uses his strength in God's service, achieving his God-given task: to "begin the deliverance of Israel from the hands of the Philistines" (Judges 13 v 5).

In his birth and death, Samson is a shadow of the Lord Jesus, whose birth was miraculous and announced by an angel, and whose death rescued his people from the grip of the devil. Yet of course, Jesus' death achieved far more than Samson's; and while Samson's story ends with his burial, Jesus rose from his grave to rule his people.

OPTIONAL EXTRA

To introduce the idea of how indistinct God's people can become from those around us, print out some "Where's Waldo?" (in the UK, "Where's Wally?") challenges from the internet. Refer back after Q7, discussing the extent to which your church is/isn't distinct from the world.

GUIDANCE ON QUESTIONS

1. Why do people disobey God? The obvious answer is: because we are sinners. But encourage people to develop that idea. Why do we like sinning? What is going on in our hearts which means we decide not to obey? Are there times we simply don't know how to obey? And so on.

2. What should happen next [in the Judges cycle], but doesn't? Israel doesn't cry out for rescue from oppression. There is no resistance to their enslavement.

- **What does this tell us about Israel's spiritual state by this time?** They have basically become pagans. They have completely adopted and adapted to the values, beliefs and idols of the Philistines. They don't cry out because they don't realize they need to—their enslavement is virtually unconscious. Israel, as a nation of God's distinctive people, are on the verge of extinction.

- **In verse 5, God begins to raise up a judge to deliver his people. Why is this remarkable, given what Israel hasn't done?** Because they haven't asked him to do this. Here, again, we see just how amazing God's love for and commitment to his people are. In the Abimelech episode, we saw God raising up a judge to save Israel from themselves. Here, he does so again, even though they haven't asked for it and (as we'll see, 15 v 9-11) don't really want one.

3. How is Samson's birth similar to Jesus' birth?

Note: If your group is less familiar with the Bible, read out Luke 1 v 26-33 before answering this question.

Both births are impossible, humanly speaking. Manoah's wife is sterile (13 v 2); Mary was a virgin (Luke 1 v 27). Both are announced by an angel (Judges 13 v 3; Luke 1 v 31). Both children have been set apart by God as his chosen ruler/rescuer (Judges 13 v 5; Luke 1 v 32-33).

4. What does the angel tell Samson's mother about how he is to be brought up (v 4-5)? As a "Nazirite." His hair is not to be cut; and even as he grows in the womb, he is not to have any alcohol, or be touched by anything unclean (and so his mother has to avoid alcohol and unclean food). See the explanation of what a Nazirite was in the Study Guide, page 32.

5. [In 14 v 1 – 16 v 3] How well does Samson keep his Nazirite vow? (hint: 14 v 10 speaks of, literally, a "drinking party.")

• 14 v 6-9: Samson touches a dead lion twice, but instead of going to the tabernacle to be cleansed so he can continue with his vow, he carries on to see the woman he likes. (His love for women comes ahead of his commitment to God.) Then he shares unclean honey (it's been in contact with a dead body) with his parents, making them unclean too.

• 14 v 10: He "made a feast" ie: held a drinking party. The implication is that he drinks alcohol, again breaking his vow.

• **How well does he keep God's commands to all his people (look back to Joshua 23 v 9-13)?** Through Joshua, God has told Israelite men not to marry women from the other nations (see also Exodus 34 v 15-16). In Judges 14 v 1-2, Samson sees a Philistine woman, and demands that his parents arrange a marriage for them. When they protest, he insists that "she's the right one for me" (v 3). By 16 v 1, Samson is sleeping with a Philistine prostitute.

Note: the issue with Samson marrying a Philistine is not that she is foreign, but that she is not a member of God's people. So Samson's parents talk about "the uncircumcised Philistines" (v 3), circumcision being the sign that a family was in relationship with God, as part of his people. They are saying: It is not right that you marry outside the covenant, as God had commanded us not to (Exodus 34 v 15-16). Why did God command this? Because he knew that Israel's men would then end up worshiping their wives' gods. This still applies to God's people today— see 2 Corinthians 6 v 14-16.

6. How do we see that Israel have essentially become Philistines:

• **in Samson's actions?** He sees no reason not to marry a Philistine, or sleep with a prostitute. Further, we see here just how violent and vengeful Philistine society is. They burn a man and his daughter—their own people—to death just to get back at Samson (15 v 6-7)! But Samson is no better—he is just as violent (he kills 30 men to get their clothes, 14 v 19), and just as driven by vengeance (15 v 7-8).

• in Judah's actions? See 15 v 9-13. Judah have no idea that God has raised up a judge to save them (v 10)—their priority is living at peace under the Philistines (v 11). They are angry with Samson for causing conflict between Israel and their enemies. And so, having discovered that God has sent someone to rescue them, they send 3,000 men to tie him up and hand him over to their enemies (v 12-13). They would rather live at peace with their enemies and worship their idols than be free to worship God. They are, essentially, no different to the Philistines.

EXPLORE MORE

Three times, we're told explicitly that Samson enjoyed Spirit-given strength (14 v 6; 14 v 19; 15 v 14-15). What does he use that strength to do each time?
• 14 v 6: To protect himself from a lion.
• 14 v 19: To kill 30 innocent men so that he can settle a bet that he has lost.
• 15 v 14-15: To escape from the Philistines, who are pursuing him because he had killed "many of them" (v 8) in order to avenge the death of his wife.

The point is that each time, his strength is used in his own interests. None of these events even begins to deliver Israel. The second and third events are caused by Samson's selfishness and pride, not by a desire to rescue his people.

... Read 1 Cor 12 v 4-7; 13 v 1-3. What does Paul say here that the Spirit gives? Gifts, for the common good (v 7).

What must these be accompanied by to stop them being useless? Love. Gifts on their own are "nothing." They must be combined with love, so that they're used in the service of God's people (13 v 1-3).

Read Galatians 5 v 19-25. What does Paul say here that the Spirit gives? Fruit (part of which is love).

Which does Samson have? Which doesn't he have? He has great gifts—superhuman strength—but little or no fruit. The Spirit is operating in him, mightily—but his personal spiritual life is a complete wreck. **Which is the sign of real spiritual growth?** Fruit, not gifts. Gifts are about doing—abilities for serving and helping others, which can very easily be used for our own ends. Fruit is about being—about who we really are. **What happens if we forget this?** We will mistake the operation of gifts for the growth of fruit, and look at how we're serving, or our God-given abilities, as proof that spiritually, all is well. The "proof" of spiritual growth and spiritual health is seeing the fruit of the Spirit growing in our characters.

7. APPLY: Why is the church adopting the values and beliefs of the world more dangerous than the world oppressing and persecuting the church? Because it's subtle; it can happen without us noticing. If you are being persecuted—eg: you lose your job because you're a Christian—you know that you are in a battle, it is obvious that you need to stand firm. But if a local or institutional church slowly, over time, simply becomes like the world, then its members will lose the battle without realizing that they need to fight. They will stop trusting and worshiping God without ever really noticing.

• How is this danger most acute in your church and your culture? The answers will, of course, vary depending on your culture, and your church.

8. How do we see Samson's weaknesses in this section [16 v 4-21]?
• *Women.* He cannot resist the women he is attracted to. By verse 9, he can't be

in any doubt about what Delilah is up to—yet he stays with her. And in verse 15, she suggests that Samson doesn't really love her (even though she doesn't love him, and is betraying him!); and Samson responds by telling her the truth. It seems he cannot bear to risk losing her, even though she is leading him to ruin.

- *Complacency.* Samson has defeated huge numbers of Philistines before; he assumes that he will be able to again and again now. Even when he, in effect, again breaks his Nazirite vow—by telling Delilah the truth, and so allowing his hair to be cut—he assumes he will still "go out as before and shake myself free" (v 21). Samson believes that he will continue to enjoy God-given strength no matter what he does, or how he uses it.

- **What, ultimately, was the key to Samson's strength (v 19-20)?** It seems that it was having uncut hair, since (v 19) it's as his hair is shaved off that "his strength left him." But verse 20 shows us a deeper answer: he was weakened because "the LORD had left him." What mattered was not so much Samson's hair, but God's presence with him. We cannot know why God chose to leave Samson to his own strength (which was, in fact, no strength at all) at this point, when he had continued to strengthen Samson as he broke other parts of his vow. But the key is that it was while God was "with" Samson that he was strong.

9. APPLY: We may think we don't believe in magic. But think about the question: *Why do I think God will bless me?* **How can we make the same mistake as:**

- **the Philistines?** By thinking: *If I do the right things—study my Bible / go to church / live rightly / pray / help my neighbor, then*

God will bless me. Or thinking: *I didn't pray before leaving for work/was rude to that person/didn't listen to the sermon properly—I'll have a bad day now.*

- **Samson?** By thinking: *Of course God will bless me. He always has done up to now, even when I've not bothered to live in obedience to him.*

- **What does it look like to live as a Christian who knows God is the God who gives graciously?** We know and enjoy the assurance that he blesses us despite, not because of, what we do. We know we can't acquire divine blessing through what we do; nor can we easily lose it through what we don't do. We know that God's favor flows from our relationship with him, not the duties we perform for him. And so all that we do—reading our Bible, praying, etc, flow out of that relationship with God, rather than being an attempt to get that favor from him. So we are neither dutiful in our obedience, nor complacent in disobedience.

10. How does Samson at last show faithful reliance on God [in verses 22-31]? He prays, humbly and relationally (v 28). He recognizes that God is "Sovereign"—the One to whom he owes obedience; and that he is LORD—the God of Israel. He asks God to "remember me"—he knows God has every right to ignore him. He does not assume that he can be strong; now he asks God to make him strong. And though he wants vengeance, he is willing to die with his enemies (v 30). This is not a self-serving request (otherwise he would have said: *Please strengthen me so I can escape*). Hebrews 11 v 32-34 says Samson was a man of faith, who in his weakness was made strong. This is the only time in his life where it could be said that Samson shows faith.

- **What does it cost him to fulfil his mission?** His life. His God-given mission was to "begin the deliverance of Israel from the hands of the Philistines" (13 v 5). This is where he shows the impotence of the Philistine god, Dagon, and kills the rulers of the Philistines. But to do so costs him his own life.

11. How does Samson's victory point us to the cross of Jesus? Both:
- were *betrayed* by someone who had acted as a friend—Delilah and Judas.
- were *handed over* to Gentile oppressors—Philistines / Romans.
- were *rejected by Israel*—Judah / the religious leaders and the crowd.
- appeared *completely crushed* by their enemies.
- *reversed the apparent triumph* of God's enemies: Dagon / Satan (see Col 2 v 15).
- were *alone* as they did their work of salvation.
- were *not asked for* (see Romans 5 v 8).
- had to *die* to win their greatest victory.

- **How is what Jesus did in his death even greater?**
  - *Why he was there:* Samson was in the temple of Dagon as a result of his own inability to live under God's rule—his downfall was brought about by his disobedience. Jesus died on the cross in obedience to God's rule—his death was a result of our disobedience, not his.
  - *What his death achieved:* Samson's death only began Israel's deliverance (we have to wait for King David, decades later, for it to be completed). Jesus' death achieved deliverance "once for all" (Hebrews 10 v 10).
  - *When he rules:* With his death, Samson's

life was over and his rule was at an end—his burial ends the story (Judges 16 v 31). Jesus did not stay buried, and rose to rule beyond his grave.

12. APPLY: What does Samson teach us about How not to follow God?! Make sure this discussion reaches conclusions which are useful for your group as Christians today (ie: not "Don't marry a Philistine"!). Samson is a good case study in many of the mistakes we make in our attitude to living as part of God's people—here are some:
- Complacency.
- Selfishness.
- Being directed by our feelings.
- An implicit resentment of the role God has given us.
- Mistaking the possession of spiritual gifts for spiritual growth.
- Using our gifts for our own ends.
- Sexual immorality.

You might like to finish by pointing out how wonderful it is that even a man like this, when he humbly prays to the LORD, is heard, answered, and used. Which is greatly encouraging for sinners like us!

- **What does the Samson episode teach us about how kind God is?** Some suggestions:
  - He rescues his people, even when they don't ask him for it because they are determined to live like those who don't know him.
  - He does the impossible for people, bringing life where there has been barrenness.
  - He does not allow his people to be completely consumed by the culture around them.
  - He uses sinful people, and even their actual sins, to achieve his good purposes for his people.

6 Judges 17 – 21
"ISRAEL HAD NO KING"

THE BIG IDEA
When we make up our own religion and rule ourselves, the results are horrendous—we need the rescuing, forgiving King Jesus.

SUMMARY
The last five chapters of Judges are different from the rest. The earlier passages give us a bird's-eye view of the state of Israel, telling us only that the people "did evil in the eyes of the LORD" (eg: 3 v 7; 10 v 6). Here, we have a ground-level, detailed view of what life was like during those times. They are two case studies on what it was that God rescued Israel *from*. They barely mention the LORD; this is what life is like when people choose to live as they see fit, rather than under God's rule.

These two episodes are horrific. We see a family and tribe who make up their own religious approach to God, and live how they want. Next, we see a town and nation who engage in awful acts, including gang rape and mass rape. Then the book ends, reminding us "Israel had no king." We are left looking to a king to rescue Israel—ultimately, we are left aching for King Jesus.

OPTIONAL EXTRA
Write a quiz about the judges, based on what you've learned during the previous five studies.

GUIDANCE TO QUESTIONS
1. If you had to sum up humans in one word, what would it be? There are many good answers to this question! We are "created"; "image-bearers"; "sinful"; "fallen"; "workers"; "worshipers," etc.

2. What is the approach of Micah and his mother in relating to God?

- **v 3:** She gives her money "to the LORD" by making an image of him. She wants to worship God through a physical object.

- **v 4:** (This is not easy to spot!) Micah has returned 1100 shekels (v 3), which his mother says she will give to God. But in v 4, she gives 200 shekels, keeping 900. She clearly thinks she can satisfy God with part of her wealth (and presumably, part of her life). She will give God just enough to win his blessing, and keep the rest for herself.

- **v 5:** Micah has made his own ephod (a way of discerning God's will).

- **v 5, 7-12:** They need a priest. Priests spoke to God and performed sacrifices on the people's behalf, and taught the people about God.

- **v 6:** Their religion makes no difference to how they live. They do as they see fit, not as God sees fit.

- **What is Micah's aim in all this (v 13)?** To get access to God so he can get God to be "good" to him (based on his definition "good"). He wants God to serve him.

3. How is this different from the way God has told his people to relate to him? If you need to, look up these verses…

⌄

Divide into pairs and give each a passage to look up, to see how God had told his people to relate to him.

- **Exodus 25 v 1-9:** God dwells among his people at the tabernacle, built just as he commanded. His presence cannot be "earned" through shrine-building.

- **Exodus 28 v 6-30:** There is one ephod and its breastplate; it is for the high priest (Aaron) to wear, in the tabernacle (which contains the Holy Place); the high priest is the one who uses it to make decisions for Israel (probably the Urim and Thummim stones were thrown, the way they fell giving the decision).

- **Exodus 20 v 4-6:** Israel is not to make any image of God. Why? Because at best, any depiction of God automatically reveals part of his nature, but conceals another. At worst, it teaches God's people that they can shape (and re-shape) God.

- **Numbers 8 v 5-15:** Only Aaron's sons can serve as priests. The Levites are to assist the priests. But Micah appoints a son as his priest (ie: anyone can now serve in this way); then finds a Levite, who is closer to the "ideal," so swaps priests.

- **Exodus 19 v 4-6:** God rescues and blesses Israel not because of their religious activity, but because of his own will. Israel had done nothing to make God rescue them from Egypt. They enjoy his blessings not by making their own religious shrines, but by faithful, humble submission to God.

The point is: this is homemade religion, structured to suit Micah and his mother, rather than God-ordained religion, carried out in obedience to his instructions. It is religion according to what is right in Micah's eyes, not what is right in the LORD's eyes.

4. What happens to Micah [18 v 1-31]?
Don't get too detailed! Look at verses 11-26. The Danite soldiers stand outside Micah's house while five of them take his shrine (v 17-18); and they convince his priest to go with them (v 19-21). When Micah challenges them, they threaten to kill him

(v 25), so he is forced to leave empty-handed (v 26).

- **What is tragic about verse 24?** All of Micah's faith is in his self-made shrine. So the Danites have taken all he has—all he looked to and relied on to give him God's favor and blessing. "What else do I have?" Micah discovered that the god he had made for himself was nothing, and could be lost in a few moments. The tragedy is that he is a member of Israel, who should have known the God whose presence cannot be stolen, and whose blessing does not rely on possessions or rituals.

⌄

- **Look up Ps 73 v 23-26.** What difference does knowing the real God make?

5. What is the Levite's career path (17 v 7-12; 18 v 18-21; 18 v 30-31)? He begins as a wanderer, having left the place he was meant to serve in (17 v 7-8). He finds a paid job (v 10-12); then goes on to work for a whole tribe (18 v 18-21). He ends up running the religious activities of Dan, in their newly-conquered city (18 v 30-31).

- **What seems to be driving his decisions?** Self-promotion. He uses ministry to boost his own status, even when that means breaking God's laws. We see this most clearly in 18 v 18-21. At first he protests at the stealing of Micah's idols—it will leave him without a shrine ie: without a job. But when he is offered the promotion of leading Dan's idol-worship, he is "glad" (v 20) and leaves with them.

- **What is tragic about the detail given about him in v 30?** He is "Jonathan son of Gershom, the son [ie: descendant] of Moses." This man is related to the greatest Israelite of all, Moses! This shows how far

Israel has fallen. A member of the greatest family is now leading idol-worship.

6. APPLY: ... How are we tempted to reshape God?

(1) By consciously, intellectually rejecting part of the Scriptural revelation of God. We do this whenever we say: *We can no longer accept a God who does this... or who forbids this...* When we use the term "no longer" we are saying: *Our culture's distaste for this idea means we must drop it!* Like Micah's family, this is reshaping God to fit our society and hearts.

(2) By simply ignoring or avoiding those aspects of revelation we don't like. For example, God is very strong on giving our money away and not spending it lavishly on ourselves. But we can just avoid thinking out the implications of this for our own lives.

(3) By making all morality subjective. Eg: two professing Christians may be having sex even though they are not married. Why? Because they prayed (good) and then "felt peace about it" (irrelevant!). They ignore the objective commands about sex and marriage God has given them in his word.

- **How might we quietly copy [Micah's] mother's approach to pleasing God (17 v 3-4)?** Most obviously, by seeing our money as "ours," and deciding (very generously, we think) to let God have some of it. But in the use of her money, Micah's mother shows that she does not want God to have sovereignty over every part of her life; that she wants to hedge her bets, relying on him but also on her money. So we copy Micah's mother whenever we claim to have Jesus as Lord, but only obey him in certain "sectors" of our lives, keeping back some money/time/emotions/relationships in case God doesn't deliver what we want.

- **How might we quietly copy the Levite's approach to ministry?** The Levite uses his ministry as an opportunity to enhance his own status. It is very easy to "do ministry" in our church to be seen; to look impressive; to grow our reputation or popularity. A good question to ask, to see if/where we are doing this, is: *Would I still joyfully and diligently do this ministry if I knew that, other than me and God, no one would ever know I had done it?*

7. [In Judges 19] How is the woman treated badly by:

- **the Levite?** (1) He has her as a concubine (v 2)—a second-class wife, a sex-slave. (2) When the men of Gibeah are outside his door, he "sent her outside to them" (v 25), to be raped and murdered. (3) He then "got up in the morning" (v 27)—he was so unconcerned that he had gone to bed while she was being attacked. He would have continued on without her had he not found her in the doorway (v 27). He speaks to her as to an animal (v 28). We really should feel revulsion at all this.

- **her father?** He "gladly welcomed" the Levite (v 3), showing him hugely generous hospitality for five days. Why is he so generous? Probably because he wants to avoid the disgrace of having a daughter who ran away from her (second-class) marriage. We are never told that the woman agrees to go with the Levite—the implication is her father sends her back.

- **the host?** He is very kind to the Levite, welcoming him in (v 16-20). But when the men outside demand to have sex with the Levite, he offers them his concubine—and his own daughter (v 24)

- **the men of Gibeah?** Their behavior is truly "wicked" (v 22), "vile" and "disgraceful" (v 23).

Each man treats women shamefully. They appear to see men as more valuable than women.

EXPLORE MORE
Read Genesis 19 v 1-11; 24-28.
What are the similarities between events in Sodom and in Gibeah?
• Strangers come to the town (angels; the Levite with his concubine and man-servant)
• Men surround the house, pound the door, and demand to have sex with a man (or men).
What happens to Sodom? In judgment, God utterly destroys it.
Gibeah is Israel's "showcase" here. So what does the similarity between Sodom and Gibeah tell us about:
• **what Israel is like?** The people of God—people given the covenants of Abraham and Moses, the law and the prophets, the tabernacle, the exodus, savior-judges—are no better than the worst of everyone else. God's people could not be any worse.
• **what Israel deserves?** Sodom deservedly bore God's anger. Gibeah deserve the same. We cannot read Judges 19 without crying out for justice for the concubine (though she wasn't totally innocent—v 2; she had been unfaithful to the Levite).

8. [In 20 v 1-17] How is the Levite's account an edited version of what really happened? In verse 5, there are three key changes/omissions to his account:
• He says "the men of Gibeah," suggesting it was all of them, rather than only "some of the wicked men" (19 v 22).
• He says they intended to kill him; in fact, they wanted to rape him (19 v 22)
• "They raped my concubine"—he omits "sen[ding] her outside to them" (19 v 25).
The point is that while the men of Gibeah are certainly villains, overtly and horrifically

sinful, so is the Levite. He looks and sounds much better/more moral; in fact, he is not.

9. What do the men of Israel do next (v 48)? They put everyone—women, children and animals—to death. It is a genocide. The whole of Benjamite society is slaughtered.

10. How do they solve the problem?
• **[21] v 5-14:** They discover (v 8-9) that the men of Jabesh Gilead didn't come to the assembly at Mizpah in ch 20. Since these men had not been there, they hadn't made the oath never to give their daughters to Benjamites. So they send a small army against this Israelite town (v 10), killing anyone who isn't a female virgin (v 11), so they can give those virgins to Benjamite men to marry (v 12-14). But (v 15) this is only a partial solution, because there aren't enough virgins to give each Benjamite survivor a wife.

• **v 15-23:** They send the Benjamites off to the annual festival of the LORD to "seize a wife from the girls" (v 19-21). Because they have been abducted, their fathers won't be oath-breakers, because they didn't choose to give their daughters to the Benjamites—they had been kidnapped (v 22). The plan "works" brilliantly (v 23).

• **Remember, all this started when a woman was raped and murdered. How are Israel's actions here desperately ironic?** To see justice done for the raped concubine (or rather, the Levite), Israel went to war with Benjamin. But in the course of this war, they killed thousands of women in cold blood. Then, to solve the problems this has created, they murder the men and marry off the women of an Israelite town, and basically cause the rape of all the virgins who lived there (who have not exactly chosen to marry the Benjamite men). Then they sponsor the abduction, and subsequent rape, of the girls at the festival. The terrible irony is that in seeking to bring justice for one rape and murder, Israel rapes and murders countless more.

11. APPLY: [The only way to avoid bitterness and resentment is to practice forgiveness.] How can we do this?

⊗

- **What is forgiveness?** Primarily it is a promise to: not bring the wrong up with the person; not bring it up with others; not bring it up in your own thoughts; not dwell on the hurt; not nurse ill-will toward the other.

If you're pushed for time, split your group into three, giving each one passage:

- **Luke 17 v 3-6:** By doing it—and expecting to do it repeatedly. Forgiveness (see the definition above) is a decision—an act of will, rather than subject to our feelings. It is granted before it is felt.

- **Matthew 18 v 21-35:** Only the knowledge of our debt to God can put in perspective someone else's debt to us. And only the knowledge that God has canceled our debt, in the costliest way possible, will enable us to cancel another's debt to us. The forgiveness of Christ gives us the emotional humility to forgive (*Who am I to withhold forgiveness when I am such a sinner?*) and the emotional resources to forgive (*What has this person's wrongdoing really robbed me of, when I have so much more in Christ?*).

- **Mark 11 v 25:** We are to forgive when someone repents (ie: seeks forgiveness from us and reconciliation with us); but

here, we are told to forgive before trying to be reconciled to someone. If we wait for repentance, we may wait a long time; and that time is ample for bitterness to grow and strangle our ability to forgive.

12. APPLY: How is Judges 21 v 25 a good summary of the book, and the central problem of humanity? Judges is about how people—even God's blessed people—live in the way they "see fit." Time and again, we have seen the people doing what seems right to them, even though it is evil in the eyes of God. These last chapters have shown us, on a personal, tribal and national level, the catastrophes this causes. So Judges is a book about how all people need saving, and ruling. Israel "had no king"—no one to lead and rule them in obeying God. Humanity's central problem is that we live as we think best, and it leads to disaster—and that we live as though there is no King, rejecting the only way our society and hearts can be purged of evil.

- **How does Judges leave us aching for King Jesus?** Just as Israel should end Judges aching for a king, so should we. Judges finishes looking towards the monarchy—the blessing that God's anointed kings would bring. In David and Solomon, we see the blessings of such a king's rule. But even their rules are flawed, and temporary, and can't deal with the evil of the people's hearts. Judges leaves us aching for a King who will deliver people without being asked to; who will choose people who haven't chosen him; who will achieve the rescue entirely himself, because we are too weak to; and who will bring the ultimate "glorious defeat" that the judges (particularly Samson) make us expect. Judges shows us how much we need Jesus!

Dig Deeper into Judges with Timothy Keller

JUDGES FOR YOU

The second in this new, ground-breaking series, Dr Keller brings his trademark insights and real-world applications to the book of Judges. Written for Christians of every age and stage, *Judges For You* is written for you to read as a book; to feed on as a daily devotional, complete with helpful reflection questions; to equip to you lead, whether preaching in church or teaching in a small group.

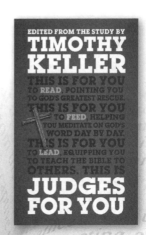

EXPLORE DAILY DEVOTIONAL

These Bible studies help you open up the Scriptures and will encourage and equip you in your walk with God. Available as a book or as an app, *Explore* features Tim's notes on Judges and other books of the Bible, alongside contributions from trusted Bible teachers including Mark Dever, Tim Chester, Mike McKinley and Ray Ortlund.

Find out more at:

www.thegoodbook.com/for-you • www.thegoodbook.co.uk/for-you
www.thegoodbook.com/explore • www.thegoodbook.co.uk/explore

Good Book Guides
The full range

1 Thessalonians:
7 Studies
Mark Wallace
ISBN: 9781904889533

2 Timothy: 7 Studies
Mark Mulryne
ISBN: 9781905564569

Titus: 5 Studies
Tim Chester
ISBN: 9781909919631

Hebrews: 8 Studies
Justin Buzzard
ISBN: 9781906334420

James: 6 Studies
Sam Allberry
ISBN: 9781910307816

1 Peter: 5 Studies
Tim Chester
ISBN: 9781907377853

1 Peter: 6 Studies
Juan R. Sanchez
ISBN: 9781784980177

1 John: 7 Studies
Nathan Buttery
ISBN: 9781904889953

Revelation 2–3: 7 Studies
Jonathan Lamb
ISBN: 9781905564682

TOPICAL

Heaven: 6 Studies
Andy Telfer
ISBN: 9781909919457

Biblical Womanhood:
10 Studies
Sarah Collins
ISBN: 9781907377532

The Holy Spirit: 8 Studies
Pete & Anne Woodcock
ISBN: 9781905564217

**Promises Kept: Bible
Overview** 9 Studies
Carl Laferton
ISBN: 9781908317933

Making Work Work:
8 Studies
Marcus Nodder
ISBN: 9781908762894

Women of Faith:
8 Studies
Mary Davis
ISBN: 9781904889526

Meeting Jesus: 8 Studies
Jenna Kavonic
ISBN: 9781905564460

Man of God: 10 Studies
Anthony Bewes & Sam
Allberry
ISBN: 9781904889977

Contentment: 6 Studies
Anne Woodcock
ISBN: 9781905564668

The Apostles' Creed:
10 Studies
Tim Chester
ISBN: 9781905564415

Experiencing God:
6 Studies
Tim Chester
ISBN: 9781906334437

Real Prayer: 7 Studies
Anne Woodcock
ISBN: 9781910307595

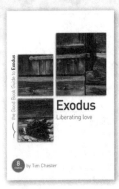

the**good**book
C O M P A N Y

Opening up the Bible

At The Good Book Company, we are dedicated to helping Christians and local churches grow. We believe that God's growth process always starts with hearing clearly what he has said to us through his timeless word—the Bible.

Ever since we opened our doors in 1991, we have been striving to produce resources that honour God in the way the Bible is used. We have grown to become an international provider of user-friendly resources to the Christian community, with believers of all backgrounds and denominations using our Bible studies, books, evangelistic resources, DVD-based courses and training events.

We want to equip ordinary Christians to live for Christ day by day, and churches to grow in their knowledge of God, their love for one another, and the effectiveness of their outreach.

Call us for a discussion of your needs or visit one of our local websites for more information on the resources and services we provide.

Your friends at The Good Book Company

NORTH AMERICA		thegoodbook.com		866 244 2165
UK & EUROPE		thegoodbook.co.uk		0333 123 0880
AUSTRALIA		thegoodbook.com.au		(02) 6100 4211
NEW ZEALAND		thegoodbook.co.nz		(+64) 3 343 2463

 WWW.CHRISTIANITYEXPLORED.ORG
Our partner site is a great place for those exploring the Christian faith, with a clear explanation of the good news, powerful testimonies and answers to difficult questions.